HOW TO HELP YOUR CHILD START SCHOOL

HOW TO HELP YOUR CHILD START SCHOOL

Bernard Ryan, Jr.

SOUNDVIEW BOOKS DARIEN, CONNECTICUT

Published by Soundview Books
100 Heights Road, Darien, Connecticut 06820

First printing, 1980

Library of Congress Cataloging in Publication Data

Ryan, Bernard Jr. 1923-
How to Help Your Child Start School

Bibliography: p.
Includes index.
1. Readiness for school.   2. Kindergarten.   3. Education, Preschool—Curricula.   I. Title
LB1132.R9   372'.21   80-50170
ISBN 0-934924-01-5

*For Jean   *   Nora Louise   *   Barbara Ann*

Acknowledgements

This book could not have been written without the responsive interest of dozens of people across the United States who generously gave the author their materials for kindergarten parents, their kindergarten curriculum guides, their answers to many questions, and their opinions on many subjects.

Particular thanks go to the following for talking with the author at length, reviewing material used in the preparation of the text, and, in some cases, welcoming the author as an observer in their schools and classrooms: Gertrude Asher, Cleo Banks, Charlotte Brody, and Lisa Hirsch, all of the Little Red School House, New York City; Dr. Lydia Duggins, professor of education, the University of Bridgeport, Bridgeport, Connecticut; Elizabeth S. Gord, principal, Decatur Elementary School, La Jolla, California; Helen Martin, principal, Ina E. Driscoll Elementary School, Wilton, Connecticut; Janet Leonard O'Loughlin, kindergarten teacher, Pound Ridge, New York; Lydia Schneid, school psychologist, Wilton Public Schools; Seymour Schneid, principal, West School, New Canaan, Connecticut; Carol Scholl, kindergarten teacher, Ina E. Driscoll School; Rose Ann Smith, librarian, Tilford W. Miller School, Wilton, Connecticut; Susan Stewart, kindergarten teacher, Sunset View Elementary School, San Diego, California; Sara

McKissock Vick, kindergarten teacher, Albion Public Schools, Albion, New York; and Nancy M. Whitcomb, kindergarten teacher, Cabrillo Elementary School, San Diego, California.

Others who were helpful include Catherine Brunner, supervisor, early childhood education, Baltimore Public Schools; Ruth E. Fiske, retired principal, Angeline M. Post School, Wilton, Connecticut; Charles P. Harris of the Council for Public Schools, Boston, Massachusetts; Marjorie Head, coordinator of dissemination, Nova Elementary School, Fort Lauderdale, Florida; Joseph B. Hill, coordinator of curriculum, San Francisco Unified School District; Grace Iacolucci, kindergarten curriculum specialist, Department of Elementary and Secondary Education, Milwaukee Public Schools; Mrs. George M. Kendall, retired teacher of English, Peterborough, New Hampshire, Public Schools; Dr. John Henry Martin of the Responsive Environments Corp., Englewood Cliffs, New Jersey; Mrs. Afton Dill Nance, consultant in early elementary education, State of California Department of Education; Dr. Helen F. Robison, Teachers College, Columbia University, New York City; Hewitt Fitts Ryan, M.D., San Diego, California; Harriet Sherman, kindergarten teacher, the Roosevelt School, Rowayton, Connecticut; Richard A. Zucker, M.D., Wilton, Connecticut.

Permission to use the diary of inch-worm observations, from the kindergarten in the San Francisco Unified School District, was given by Joseph B. Hill, coordinator of curriculum, teacher Edith Van Orden, and Ruth Tisdale, who prepared the report.

For the material on developmental ages, in the last chapter, I am indebted to Miss Jacqueline Haines of the Gesell Institute and an informal talk she gave to parents of students at the Ina E. Driscoll Elementary School in Wilton, Connecticut.

BR, Jr.

Contents

Introduction

Schools and children: no two alike.

The purpose of this book is to help you and your child toward an awareness of what school is and an expectation of what it can be.

No two children are alike.

They may look similar. They may have had similar experiences. They may be the same age. They may reflect the same social and economic backgrounds. But no two children who are ready for school are exactly the same.

Neither are any two schools.

Schools today look very much alike. You can step into a kindergarten classroom anywhere in the United States and find the same materials and equipment you saw in the last one you peeked into. Teacher training, also, is much the same everywhere, so that the same basic knowledge and skills have been imparted to most teachers. But the ways in which that training is put to use and the experience that has been applied on top of it vary almost as much as humanity varies.

School is a very special place, and kindergarten is probably where your child will have his or her first formal educational experience. Going to school is the single most important continuing event in a child's life, lasting anywhere from twelve to twenty years. The experiences of the first year in school in kindergarten will be the foundation for all that follows.

Your unique child.

Your child is a very special person—a unique person. No other human being—even an identical twin—has ever grown at exactly the same rate, developed physical abilities at precisely the same age, or experienced just the same events. No one else will ever again use precisely the same timetable or follow exactly the same steps.

Now this unique person, your child, is ready to put together all the growing, development, and experiences of the first five years and set off to school. It will be an enormous advantage if he or she has already absorbed the knowledge that school is a special place where each pupil is wanted and respected as a special person, that school is where one learns to read for pleasure and satisfaction as well as useful information, that school provides opportunities to use materials and equipment to achieve worth-while purposes, that, in sum, school—and learning—are exciting.

It is the intention of this book to help you tell your child that school is that special place and to help you understand how school will make learning exciting. Such an intention encompasses a fourfold purpose:

☐ to describe the characteristics of your child at this stage;
☐ to describe the tasks to be faced in the first year of school;
☐ to help your child understand what will happen in school;
☐ to help you understand why it will happen.

It is not the aim of this book to give you an itemized list of characteristics to look for in your child. Characteristics developed in clinical detail and by laboratory reports are better described by Gesell and other psychologists at the Gesell Institute and elsewhere who have devoted lifetimes to watching small fry through one-way mirrors. However, you will probably recognize in your child many of the characteristics described in these pages.

Generally, throughout the book, the characteristics described are those of "normal" or average five-year-olds. By the same token, the attributes discussed in describing both schoolrooms and teaching techniques will represent a composite of those found in many schools in many parts of the United States today.

The tasks facing your child in the first year of school are indeed *tasks*. It is a job of work to adjust to spending several hours in a room with upward of twenty people when you have previously had to cope with only a handful or less, to answer to a strange new authority when you have spent a lifetime training one or two grownups to respond to your beck and call, to absorb in a few months the basic concepts and disciplines of learning that the human race has been developing since history began, and to make your mental, emotional, social, and physical health and well-being just as sound as the next person's.

What happens—and why.

Your child is able to understand what will happen in school. Undoubtedly he or she has learned to anticipate future events, whether as incidental as a trip to the store or a weekend at Grandma's or as earth-shaking as the arrival of a sibling. The more understanding your child gains in anticipating *what* is going to happen in school, the less upsetting will be the event.

You, on the other hand, need to know the *why* of what happens. Your "why" must be a well-informed "why" if you are going to continue to help your child understand what is happening and if you are going to be able to evaluate his or her progress.

The purpose of this book, then, is to help you help your child, both now at the start of school and for long years ahead, to become an active participant in the learning process.

"He" or "him"—in Kindergarten.

Some arbitrary decisions are necessary for purposes of clarifying the text. First, your child will be called "he" or "him" throughout most of this book. This is not a matter of chauvinism but of convenience, and no slight to girls is intended. I believe this style is more individualized than "they" or "them" and less cluttered and annoying than saying "he or she" over and over again. Kindergarten teachers, on the other hand, will be referred to as "she" and "her," as the overwhelming majority is female.

Second, the "working model" used for demonstration and example will be the year of school that comes first in the lives of the majority of boys and girls now growing up in the United States—the kindergarten. There are, of course, some children in this country who begin school as early as the age of three in a private nursery, play group, or other preschool program, and there are many who begin at the age of six in a public-school first grade. However, the majority first go to school in a public kindergarten sometime after their fourth birthdays and before their sixth. Therefore the child in this text is *about* five years old. He may already have celebrated his fifth birthday, or he may be four going on five. Probably he is nearer to his fifth birthday than to his fourth or sixth.

In areas where the public-school system does not offer a kindergarten program, this text is pertinent to the school experience offered early in the first grade, since first grade must make up for the lack of kindergarten experience. In any case, an understanding of what kindergarten is may create a desire among parents to urge local authorities to provide public kindergartens if there are none in the vicinity.

The emphasis in this book is on program and content. Places and objects are incidental to the substance of the first year of school. What is learned and how it is learned are what count, not where the doll corner and block corner are. Therefore, countless places and objects will be mentioned or described, but always for the purpose of making a point about the school program and its content.

This book—in brief.

Part One provides some background on your child's fifth year of development, needs, intelligence, and senses. It then goes into a brief history of kindergartens and the basic objectives of kindergarten schooling, with a discussion of some misconceptions frequently found among the parents of beginning school children. The physical plant—school and classroom—is described, as is the well-structured social system they contain. Getting ready for school and all it entails for your child within himself, within the home, and away from home are described next. Part One ends with some comment on various private and public preschool programs and some practical notes about registration and getting to kindergarten.

Part Two will take you, moment by moment, through a typical day in school so that you can describe it to your child.

Part Three takes you in some depth into the learning experiences in school. It talks about learning concepts and the basic cultural elements that one person learns from another and about the fun your child will get from discovery. It details coming experiences with creative materials, language and literature, social studies, science and nature, number concepts, music, and health, safety, and physical education.

Part Four explores the continuing help in growth and development that you can give your child at home throughout the school year. It presents the teacher's background and training role in evaluating your child's progress, and conferences with you. This section also plunges into that famous word "readiness," to give you, in some depth, a picture of your child's general readiness, skill in communications, and numerical and handwriting readiness as he approaches the end of the first year of school and the completion of his own foundation for all future learning.

A short final section offers some things to think about: typical patterns of developmental behavior and comments from teachers, principals, and others who have closely observed what happens to children in the first year of school.

Lastly, a word of advice. Although it is important for you to be informed and knowledgeable about your child's first year of school, the most important thing you can do is to relax and enjoy it—for then he can go and do likewise.

Part One

Your Schoolgoer and the School

1

The Year of Shaping and Molding

On a plateau at five.

As your child reaches the age of five, the first intensive growth period is slackening. He is slowing down and reaching a plateau in growth and development. Body and brain have raced to multiply in size and ability, and by now he has gained the primary achievement of motor development: the ability to control his body. Since, fundamentally, all behavior is motor behavior, he can be proud of a major accomplishment.

However, he couldn't care less. He is not going to stop to marvel that his physical skills have resulted from a combination of natural maturation and learning. If you tell him that he has learned to see, you will make no impression whatever. Yet the growth of his vision—as yet only about 75 per cent complete—helps greatly to account for the development of his perceptual skills, which give him the ability to understand the world around him and which are the logical starting point of all learning. He has developed a sense of laterality, with which his mind distinguishes between the two sides of his body and gives him an inner sense of his own symmetry. He has learned to project his laterality into space, giving himself what psychologists call directionality. Laterality combines with directionality to produce co-ordination, enabling arms and legs to throw or catch a ball or ride a tricycle, hands to draw or scribble with a crayon, and eyes to focus near or far. His vision is, in a sense, the totality of his motor-perceptual skills.

By now: spatial discrimination.

With this co-ordination, he has learned to perform a neat trick. For four or five years, he has been perceiving the qualities of things through his senses: hard or soft, rough or smooth, wet or dry to his touch; loud or quiet, harsh or musical to his hearing; bright or dark, red or blue to his sight; sweet or sour to his taste; delicate or pungent to his nose. All this time, by combining and analyzing the information from his five senses on the qualities of things, he has been recognizing forms; he has been developing form perception. But that is not all. Although everything in the world he lives in is somehow related in space, space is not a quality but a concept. Your child, then, has learned to perceive forms through his senses and to interpret their relationships in terms of a concept he cannot truly see, touch, taste, hear, or smell. He has developed spatial discrimination—a useful accomplishment that your five-year-old has probably been doing for half a lifetime.

From laterality and directionality to co-ordination, from co-ordination to form perception and spatial discrimination have been giant steps in your child's early learning process and in the development of his motor and perceptual skills. On top of them he has piled mounds of information gathered in his every waking hour. Much of this information he has organized into relationships, and some of it into concepts more intricate and subtle than the vast one of space.

The family is now familiar—but here comes 'work'.

One of these relationships and concepts is his family. Into the ever-expanding reservoir of his computerlike brain he has "programed" thousands of details of each one of you and of life as it is lived by all of you together. Like the well-programed computer, which can retrieve the proper information if you ask for it properly, his mind tells him what to expect when almost any button is pushed. In a word, he is pretty familiar with the people of the family and the family situation.

Now he is to be thrust out of the familiar and out of the home. He is to enter an entirely new environment, and for probably the first time (unless he has been in a preschool program) he is to be surrounded by a peer group. Until now, most of those around him for long periods of time have been older, and perhaps one or two have been younger. Now all but one or two will be the same age as he is. In addition, the pattern of daily life will be different, alternating between home and family and the outside world and its atmosphere of "work." That outside world will require a physical thrust on his part into a world of activities that demand neuromuscular skills he may not yet have developed. It will also require a mental thrust into a world of concepts, logic, symbolism, and communications of which he has not yet dreamed. It is a big order.

Luckily, it comes at just the right moment. As he approaches or reaches the age of five, your child has probably reached a balance, a state of equilibrium, in several ways. He is less rampant, loud, and defiant than the four-year-old who succeeded your co-operative and easy-going three-year-old. He is likely to start a job and stay with it under his own motivation. He likes to discuss things at length, and may have become a philosopher. He is discovering his individuality, and for a while now he will be content to stay within the bounds of that individuality, well-adjusted and secure, calm and friendly. He probably likes to do things for you and to please you, and he will transfer that appreciation of authority to his teacher.

These are broad and general characteristics. The total effect of the first year of school will develop out of the interplay of the physical, emotional, social, and mental characteristics of the children, of the school, and of his out-of-school experiences. You can see some of that interplay if you consider some of the needs of your five-year-old.

What your five-year-old needs.

He needs, for instance, a friendly teacher and a rather homelike classroom. Emotionally, he is now prone to unreasoning fears of new situations. He depends on the love and approval of all adults, and his strong emotional link with home gives him a great need to belong. Familiar routines give him needed security. He likes to know what is expected of him, and he responds well to praise and fair treatment.

Above all else, he needs to talk and to manipulate ideas. He needs opportunities to explore and understand the world around him. Mentally, he is eager and curious. His attention span is short; his interest is in the here and now. He is getting new ideas, seeing new relationships, adding to his vocabulary, which probably ranges from fifteen to twenty-five hundred words. He likes to hear stories read aloud and probably can repeat them in sequence. He can think things through and solve simple problems.

He needs much freedom and physical activity. He is full of energy but tires easily. His large muscles are ahead of his small muscles in developing, but both need strengthening. Running, jumping, climbing, dancing, and rhythmic play are as important as block building, puzzles, cutting, and drawing. Probably he is still rather farsighted, and though he has good speech he may still show some infantile articulation. His hearing by now is fairly acute, and probably he has developed right-handedness or left-handedness. If he has had comparatively little social life, he has built up very little immunity, and is susceptible to colds and other respiratory infections and to communicable diseases.

He needs help in working with others. Socially, the discovery of his individuality has led to relative independence. Probably he plays well with one or two other children, but difficulties may arise when a third and fourth enter the scene. He needs the experiences of working in a group and of working independently; and, in the course of a school day, both needs must be met. He is self-centered and likes to be first, but he is learning to be tactful and to listen without interrupting and is beginning to sense himself as one of many.

The intelligence: spongelike.

The most rapid growth of intelligence occurs in the first five years of life. For most children, this is a period of spontaneous learning. In the rapture of excitement that bursts over them continuously as all their senses devour a world they have never seen before, they are like great sponges. The world bombards them with impressions and entertainment and information in endless confusion. If their excitement is not crimped, if their eagerness is not stultified by their particular environment, they somehow sort out the confusion by asking questions and getting answers. The result is knowledge, embraced without compulsion or premeditation.

They learn also subconsciously that knowledge is tentative and impermanent. It is never final and definitive but is always subject to change. What they know is not only constantly multiplying, it is also constantly being revised as new information comes in. With the continuous bombardment of new impressions and information, your child's concepts of space and of family have been revised a thousand times to include new factors and other concepts, many of them social, economic, and geographic. He understands visiting, traveling, and moving; he knows the supermarket and the ten-cent store like the back of his own hand, and he understands buying, selling, and "too expensive."

Much of this knowledge has come through verbal experiences. Our highly verbal civilization has presented your child with a mass of symbolic material. You were exposed to this phenomenon the first time your three-year-old stood up in a shopping cart, reached for the shelf and shouted gleefully or demandingly, "Jello!" He was, in fact, reading.

Reading from TV.

He learned to read from television. Not from Captain Kangaroo or from cartoons but from the commercial advertisements. In fact, you have probably noticed that he has paid much closer attention to the commercials than to the entertainment content of most programs. This is because his innate eagerness to learn is catered to by the structure of the commercials. Objects are shown in simple, clear close-up while they are described by an insistent voice, and big, simple words fill the screen while they are repeated over and over for the ear. Three-year-old eyes that are still farsighted welcome the big words and the big objects, and a receptive mind learns to read. "Sesame Street" has also helped your child to recognize letter shapes.

Television has provided your child with more than an early reading experience with supermarket words and Big Bird. If he is an average youngster, he has spent upward of three thousand hours before the picture tube. Through his eyes and ears he has been hooked up to a worldly nervous system outside his own body. He has been there—everywhere—just as you were there when man first stepped onto the moon. For television is instantaneous; it is happening contemporaneously with the events themselves.

This is true even if what you are seeing and hearing is a forty-year-old movie, for the information is not being translated or broken down into printed symbols on the page for your mind to perceive and retranslate into imagined experience. Rather, by and large, television is there, where the event is. It invites participation and involvement, and the rapidly growing, spongelike intelligence of the preschooler soaks it all up at once.

This may be the single most important factor for you to keep in mind as your child goes off to school. For you, the parent, are bringing up the rear of a parade of generations that began when Gutenberg invented movable type. You are among the last who had to learn involvement through abstract, fragmented symbols. Your child is not the very first—you yourself were among the first—for whom there was always television, but he is close to the head of the line. Whether you knew it or not, or intended it or not, he has learned to perceive an experience instantaneously, as it happens, and all his senses have learned that they can be involved.

The senses want to learn.

Your child's senses want to participate. They seek involvement and they want to learn. As they absorb the vicarious experiences and the bombardment of information that come to them, these same senses are under great pressure to make their owner grow up and learn much and learn it early. The adult world, consumed in a thousand ways with doubt and tension, is applying constant pressure on its offspring to cope. The offspring, perceiving its experiences instantaneously and seeking complete involvement, is aware of the doubts and tensions of the adult world. The information is constantly fed to your child in the form of commuting fathers who cannot get home for dinner, working mothers, sitting grandmothers, broken homes, and job changes that mean packing and moving. It is on the picture tube, as the real violence of terrorism and urban riots or as the dramatized violence of entertainment programs, as well as the obvious commercial messages that emphasize such problems as coping with tension headaches and unsure dentures, producing laundry neither soft nor white, and the more subtle doubts about feeding the family.

This, then, is your five-year-old: a complex of perceptual and motor skills, of accumulated information and refined conceptual knowledge, capable of instantaneous experience, seeking complete involvement, and at the same time reaching for his own physical, social, mental, and emotional maturity.

This is the child you are soon to see disappear through a doorway into an entirely new environment.

2

The Objectives of Kindergarten

Kindergarten is not a prep school for first grade. Nor is it a reform school where bad habits made in younger years may be straightened out. Nor is it a receiver-in-bankruptcy for the home, the church, and the community. Yet there is always a parent somewhere who expects kindergarten to be one or more of these things.

Kindergarten should be a place for your child to be valued for what he is and to be helped to prepare to cope with the world as it is and as it seems likely to be. The school's job is to know the world as it is and as it seems likely to be, but above all to know today's child. Good teaching at any level involves an exploration and evaluation of what a child—your child or any child—knows before a lesson is presented. Such an appraisal of knowledge and learning aptitude is extremely important if the kindergarten is to be, as it must be, a place where your child can be helped to flourish in all phases of his development.

Plato had the idea.

Though the word, meaning "children's garden," goes back only about 130 years, the idea of early childhood education goes back to Plato, who advised the community that it was responsible for educating its young. His ideal commonwealth included a community nursery. Long after his time, in the fifteenth century, Vittorino da Feltre established in Mantua, Italy, a school that had many of the characteristics of modern kindergarten education. He called for physical activities, pleasant surroundings, alternating periods of play and study to combat fatigue and boredom. He believed that school should be fun and that teachers should recognize the individual differences in children and lead rather than coerce them. In the seventeenth century, a Moravian bishop named John Amos Comenius, who had taken charge of a school in Poland, wrote *The Great Didactic*. He urged the teacher of young children to appeal to the child's sensory perceptions and to use material based on the child's own experiences.

But it really began with Pestalozzi, Froebel and Schurz.

French philosopher Jean-Jacques Rousseau, a century later, studied the needs of children and spoke strongly of their rights. He fought the tendency of the times to consider them as miniature adults and insisted that each age had its own characteristics and needs. He was followed within a few years by a Swiss teacher, Johann Heinrich Pestalozzi, who conducted an institute at Yverdon. He saw the value of sensory impressions in teaching young children and said that the child must be given many experiences with things before he has verbal instruction. Among the teachers at Pestalozzi's institute was Friedrich Froebel, a German who later began a school for young children in which play, games, songs, and other activities dominated. He invented the name "kindergarten" and developed a curriculum in which various materials, such as colored balls, cubes, cylinders, and spheres introduced the child to counting, combining, and dividing, while other materials were manipulated in modeling, drawing, sewing, and coloring. There was little of the free play or free creativity we take for granted today, but Froebel was the first teacher to provide developmental activities as we know them.

In the United States, the first kindergarten was established in Watertown, Wisconsin, in 1856, by a pupil of Froebel, Mrs. Carl Schurz. It was a German-speaking school for the children of immigrants. Four years later, Elizabeth Peabody started an English-speaking kindergarten in Boston. The first public kindergarten was founded in the St. Louis school system in 1873. These American kindergartens were designed mainly to serve the underprivileged. They established daily routines for the children, and they functioned as charity or social-welfare agencies for parents who were laborers.

Then came Dr. Maria Montessori.

One famous kindergarten in the twentieth century sprang from a laboring or underprivileged neighborhood. In 1907, in Rome, Dr. Maria Montessori opened a school for the children of working mothers—children who had previously been allowed to run wild in the streets. She insisted on the adaptation of schoolwork to the individual child and designed materials with which, from the age of three, children could work independently and correct their own mistakes. She emphasized the training of the senses as an introduction to reading, writing, and arithmetic, and her influence continues today in special "Montessori method" schools throughout the world.

Discovering the steps to maturity.

The most brilliant educational philosopher in the United States, John Dewey, was a contemporary of Dr. Montessori. From his experimental elementary school at the University of Chicago, established in 1896, he preached the idea that education is not preparation for life but a process of living, for man is continually confronted with new situations and must continually learn. The child, he said, lives in the present and constantly enriches his experience by readjusting to the increasing complexities of his environment. It is the school's role to provide a social environment reflecting the activities of the adult world in a modified form that children can understand, so that they learn through direct, meaningful experience. It is a matter, he said, of "discovering the steps that intervene between the child's present experience and richer maturity."

Early in the second half of the twentieth century, the emphasis of kindergarten was on experiences and activities and the "development" of the child in physical, social, and emotional ways, with intellectual growth considered a by-product. Today, however, mental or intellectual growth has begun to be recognized as equally important, and there is a growing interest in *content* as well as in experiences and activities at the kindergarten level.

Some wrong ideas that parents have.

Certain misconceptions about the objectives of kindergarten arise from this interest in intellectual growth and from the anxiety of well-meaning parents who wonder if their children are being prepared to cope with an increasingly technical and complex society. Many parents, concerned with the knowledge explosion, assume that by stuffing more information into our youngsters at an earlier age we can better prepare them for the world they will have to live in. When they look into kindergarten, they are unhappy if they do not find formal lessons complete with phonics, number and speech drills, workbooks and worksheets. Others look for worksheets and charts which are supposed to provide something they have heard and read about called "readiness," and these parents are especially pleased when they hear that "readiness tests" are being administered. If the children in the room appear to be "well controlled" and if the day appears to be "well organized," so much the better. What such parents fail to realize is that the teacher in such a room may be manipulating the children like puppets.

Happy confusion and smiling faces, with clever things made and cute things said by the children, are an equally inaccurate measure of the quality or objectives of kindergarten. Yet many parents observe a pretty room and pleasant teacher and go away pleased. Still others go the whole hog and advocate laissez faire. They are delighted if they find unlimited freedom and complete permissiveness in the kindergarten.

The right idea: Find a pathway.

The ideal kindergarten objectives are oriented neither to subject matter nor to permissiveness. They are aimed, rather, at finding a pathway between your child's present understandings and his future aptitude and ability to seek and gain knowledge. Since the child learns through experiencing, and since he experiences through his senses, that pathway is found in learning experiences that are primarily sensory. The goal of kindergarten, therefore, is to plan and provide such experiences, directing rather than suppressing or giving free rein to your child's energy. Experiences with people, with events, and with materials, experiences that nurture your child's physical, mental, social, and emotional development in firsthand, sensory ways— these are the foundation which the first year of school provides and upon which the future years will build. If your school is not kidding itself or you, these experiences are defined as learning experiences, not "prelearning," for there can be no such thing as "prelearning," when learning itself begins in the experience of the womb. No one ever got ready to learn. We live and learn.

Plan learning experiences.

The first objective of kindergarten, then, is to know your child and his present understandings. The second objective is to plan learning experiences for him. Then there are other objectives, including such generalized goals as providing a safe, healthy, and happy school environment; developing and maintaining co-operation in adjustment and in evaluation between school and home; and knowing your child as he is and the world as it is and is likely to be.

A few specific goals of kindergarten may be stated: helping your child to become aware of his physical needs by learning healthful habits of play, rest, and eating and by building his co-ordination, strength, and physical skills; helping him to gain some understanding of his social world by learning to work and play fairly in it and by developing responsibility and independence; helping the growth of his sense of accomplishment and self-esteem and the development of sound mental health; helping his understanding of his natural environment and of spatial and number relationships to develop; helping him to enjoy his literary and musical heritage, to express his thoughts and feelings creatively through language, movements, art, and music, and to observe, experiment, discover, think, generalize, and conceptualize.

These goals are achieved through informal programing and with a minimum of such academic pressure as testing and marking. The sum of these specific goals and of the chief one—to plan and provide learning experiences—is a very simple objective: to treat your child as an individual, concentrating on him as he is at this precise moment, with his particular personality and problems. The emphasis is on the fullness of his living here and now.

Nongraded schools in some cities.

In some of the larger school systems in the United States—those of St. Louis and Chicago, among others—there is one very special objective of the kindergarten year. It is to introduce the child into an elementary school that is not divided into the traditional grades. Such nongraded schools have rebelled against the idea that growth and development and "readiness" come automatically, like the daffodils of spring, just in time for testing and promotion to a higher level. Instead, they group their pupils mainly on progress in reading and advance them, during their first several years in school, in upward stages along the continuum of learning to read. Report cards are eliminated and conferences between parents and teacher take their place. In such nongraded schools, the children are grouped not by age or size but according to ability and achievement.

Certain private schools make it one of their objectives not to use the word "kindergarten" at all. The Montessori schools, for example, which have been enjoying a revival in recent years, group ages three to six together because, among other things, the older ones learn by helping the younger ones.

The things you can find in a Kindergarten room.

Forty square feet indoors and one hundred square feet outdoors—that is the measure in most states for how much space your child should have in classroom and schoolyard in his first year of school. That means a classroom 30 by 40 feet for every 30 children. Into that space, with its ceiling height of nine or ten feet, goes an astounding accumulation of equipment and materials, ranging from a movable piano to one or two toilets, from several painting easels to several hundred assorted building blocks, from one "cubby" or locker for each child to one chair apiece and several tables.

While classrooms vary to some degree, the equipment in almost all of them is organized into areas or centers of interest. One of the most important is simply floor space, wide and warm, free of drafts and obstructions, for use in games, rhythmic activities, group meetings, and rest periods. A sand table, wheel toys, and large blocks and boards, with some kind of climbing apparatus, provide physical activity. The music center includes the piano, a record player, and storage for records, music books, and rhythm instruments.

Doll corner? Maybe.

In a corner is the playhouse area or doll corner, with its kitchen stove, refrigerator and sink, table and chairs, rocking chair, chest of drawers, and doll bed. (In kindergartens that have a high proportion of children who have had a full year, or even two years, of preschool experience, you probably will not find a doll corner; "when they've had a lot of nursery school, they've been doll-cornered to death," says one teacher, "and by kindergarten it brings out the worst in them—they start pouring imaginary soup over each other's heads.")

Nearby is the play store, with shelves for supermarket products and counter for buying and selling. The book area includes bookshelves, table and chairs, and space for a large group at story time. An aquarium and herbarium, with fish and animals and live plants as well as collections of rocks and shells, are found in the science center, with a counter for simple lab work. Block building and storage demand plenty of space, with shelves one foot deep and floor space where construction may not only expand but may remain undisturbed from day to day for completion or for use in dramatic play. A workbench and storage for tools, lumber, and paint make up the woodwork center, while audiovisual facilities call for a daylight screen and cork board for pictures, with storage for slide projector and slides.

Games and manipulative materials have an area, too, where beads and strings, pegs and boards, puzzles and lottos, are used and stored. Alphabet and number materials, such as magnetic and felt letters and numerals, are usually found. The creative arts center needs wide shelves for paper storage, a Formica-top counter and sink, several double easels, storage space for clay and paint, drying space for finished work, cork board for displays. The teacher must have a desk and a closet for coat and personal belongings. All this must be accommodated within roughly 30 by 40 feet.

200 lbs. of clay, 24 qts. of paint.

In the course of the year large quantities of materials move through these areas, including 200 pounds of clay and 24 dozen crayons, 10 pounds of flour and a dozen pounds of nails, 24 quarts of poster paint, 3,000 sheets of 18- by 24-inch unprinted newspaper and hundreds of sheets of construction paper, tagboard, mounting board, and tissue paper, plus a couple of gallons of paste, 8 pounds of plasticine, 200 pounds of sand, 100 or more assorted pieces of soft wood, a dozen or so balls and hanks of yarn, and more than 4,000 paper cups, plates, and napkins and 15 cartons of straws. This is not a comprehensive list but a typical sampling.

When these furnishings and materials are compiled as you have just read them, you may visualize something resembling an overstocked warehouse. But when they are organized into centers of interest and activity by a teacher who knows their significance, they become the physical setting for a year-long series of learning experiences that are exciting and meaningful.

It's a complete social system, too.

Into this physical setting come, ideally, twenty boys and girls. Enrollment may run as high as twenty-five to produce, with the usual number of daily absences, an average attendance of twenty or so. More than that becomes a crowd. Yet, in crowded schools and in many localities where state aid to local districts for kindergarten is not the same as for grades 1 through 12 or where kindergarten is provided by local option, overcrowding often occurs and many kindergartens find themselves with an enrollment as high as forty or fifty in each classroom.

A crowded classroom creates problems for teacher and children. There is too much lining up, too much waiting, too much keeping quiet. Five-year-olds like to cluster in groups of three to five, and four or five such clusters are wieldy for the teacher and comfortable for the entire class.

Within a very few days after they begin to attend school, the members of this group become (though only their teacher is aware of it) a well-organized social system, with certain unwritten rules of formality and informality, an understood range of acceptable behavior, and a group identity and orientation.

It begins in the first day or two as responsibility. If you want a definition of the word, think of it literally: a response is an answer, and responsibility is answerability. It works three ways, for your child begins to answer to himself, to the group, and to his teacher or other authorities. Almost the first thing the teacher says the first day is, "Find something to play with." Soon every pupil knows that when he arrives he is responsible for getting himself busy at something. When it is time to put things away, each is responsible for cleaning up the materials he has been using. At the same time, responsibility to the group begins. Fred is in charge of paper, and must see that each classmate has a sheet when the teacher wants paper passed out. At snack time, Jane is in charge of paper cups, Hank in charge of straws, Vickie in charge of paper napkins. And the teacher makes sure that someone runs an errand to the office every day until all know their way and understand their responsibility to authority.

No group awareness yet.

Such development of simple responsibility leads the way toward the complex idea of co-operation among free individuals, which is the essence of a democratic society. Your child has no real interest, at this stage, in group norms or in any other aspect of the group. The desire to belong to the group is a developed condition, not a natural one, and many kindergartners have not yet become group-minded. They are in the process of becoming group-oriented, anxious to be members of the group but not yet aware of responsibilities to the group. So they must be brought to an awareness both of rules of procedure for formal and organized class activities and of general expectations for informal or individual activity. This means, for instance, that when a free-play period is over and everybody except your child has put away his game or puzzle or blocks, the entire class may be held waiting, hopefully and probably with patience, while they watch him put his things away. It also means that when the teacher is conducting some formal activity and your child says he "doesn't want to," he may not be required to do what everybody else is doing but he will be required to watch them do it rather than go do what he wants to do independently.

Quarreling is a stage in social development. Sometimes it brews up where language is not yet well enough developed to settle differences. When it explodes into physical violence or aggression, it is sometimes a test of the environment and sometimes a release of hostility and frustration. It is seldom prolonged, and even violent quarrels are quickly forgotten and often serve to cement friendships. Early in the year, the teacher accepts a wide range of such behavior, from verbal to overt aggression. Later, most members of the class know without thinking about it the difference between required, acceptable, and unacceptable behavior.

Most of the leadership toward group goals has to come from the teacher. While some of the children may be aggressive, they do not always influence others to follow them. The group in general is not ready for leadership by its peers. It is ready, however, to make some decisions about group goals. These may range from whether to celebrate Susie's birthday at snack time or at the end of the day to whether to study farms or firehouses as the next class project. However, an awareness of consensus is as foreign to the beginning kindergartner as is the general awareness of group norms, and it must be introduced and developed. From the exercise of simple decision-making powers, a group identity begins to emerge. If you can take the time to visit your child's classroom as well as some other classroom early in the year and revisit each one late in the year, you will almost literally "see" this group identity. You will realize that it would be destroyed if the two classes were abruptly intermingled and then divided into reorganized groups. In fact, such group identity has been known to disappear when a teacher was replaced, without warning or transition for the children, during the course of the year.

Who goes to Kindergarten?

The age of eligibility for kindergarten comes generally between the fourth and the sixth birthday but varies from state to state and locally from school system to school system. In Houston, Texas, your child must reach his fifth birthday by September 1 if he is to be admitted in September, while in Bridgeport, Connecticut, he may turn five as late as the following January 1. Most schools expect their kindergartners to reach five by the end of December following the opening of school, but with interviews and special testing will take older fours whose birthdays come in the winter months.

You will find some public kindergartens in every state in the Union. In many states, however, kindergarten operates by local option with local money—that is, without state aid. If you find kindergarten available to your child where there is no state aid, you can thank the wisdom of city, town, or county school district.

It is not always possible for you to get what is coming to you under the law. Although New York State law "entitles" every five-year-old to attend a free public school in the district in which he lives, state aid does not support kindergarten on the same basis as it supports the other grades. The result is that a number of school districts, especially in New York City, do not have room for all who want to go to kindergarten. Where there is no public kindergarten, or no room for your child in the public kindergarten, a strict interpretation of the New York State law means that you may enroll your five-year-old in first grade. (In effect, the law says six-year-olds *must* go to school, and five-year-olds are "entitled" to.)

'Mainstreamers' are included.

In 1976, Congress passed the Education for All Handicapped Children Act. It encourages integrating or "mainstreaming" handicapped children into regular classes wherever possible. It means that your child will have an enriching opportunity previously denied to many "normal" children: the opportunity to know someone his own age who is blind or deaf or walks lamely, if at all. Teachers report that the act has proved to be a very effective way for children at kindergarten age to learn to be helpful naturally rather than artificially. The acceptance level for the handicapped among their five-year-old peers is, they say, far higher than among adults. And, like the nonhandicapped child, the handicapped is least self-conscious at this age. So the opportunity for an excellent learning experience works two ways.

3

Getting Ready for School

The wonder of discovery.

Corny as it sounds, it is true that the world is a bright, shiny, and new place to each human being as he comes along and discovers it. It is recreated each time it is perceived, and your child has been recreating it, through all his senses, from the time four or more years ago when he discovered his toes, until now when he asks why he has to go to school and why you cannot go, too.

One of his biggest discoveries has been language. For him it has been exciting to find out what words mean, how they are strung together, and how to make them work for him. Mastering a new word or phrase has made him feel good, and his growing ability to express his experiences in words has combined with increasingly complex experiences to give him real exhilaration. You have witnessed this more than once as you realized what a chatterbox you had on your hands after he had been to a new place or done a new thing.

He has been "getting ready," of course, for a long time, in everything he does. Now, in the weeks or months before he goes off to school, you can help guide this energetic sense of discovery in ways that will prepare your child for the physical, social, emotional, and intellectual development that will continue and prosper in the coming year. But, please, do not think of yourself as a teacher or of getting ready for school as a program of instruction.

Beware of overteach and guarantees.

There is real danger lurking in what we may call the "overteach." If your child gets the idea that things are being programed into him, that "everyone knows this" except him and so he had better get with it, his sense of wonder and his joy in discovery will be severely curtailed.

Nor should you strive to make him The Perfect Child or the ideal matriculating kindergartner. You can buy kits that "guarantee" to make your preschooler learn to read and write, and books that tell you how to produce a superior mind in your offspring, and you can read books and articles that set norms and describe patterns of behavior to which you may be tempted to aspire on behalf of your youngster. But the facts are that no human being is just like another and that none can be pigeonholed. The mind that has been structured or manipulated or controlled, at any age, has been brainwashed. If you think you can decide what perfection is to be for your child's mind, you are not helping, you're hurting your child.

Therefore it is not a question of overhauling and chromium-plating your child in order to deliver a perfect little learner at the schoolhouse door. Rather, it is one of encouraging basic habits and sensitivities that will be useful in the development of a specific person and in helping normal, natural growth to continue. Such encouragement takes place within the self, within the home, and within the world beyond the home.

Important: freedom and choice.

The fundamental aspect of human intelligence is the knowledge of a *self* that is separate and distinct from the objective world. This knowledge began at birth, when your baby started enjoying the first of all freedoms—the freedom to be. By his own free movements and sensations he began to perceive the world of reality. He began to experience. He has reached toward and valued those experiences that have enhanced his world and made it more attractive to him, and he has avoided and reacted against those experiences that have not enhanced his world. Thus he has learned the two basic conditions for the knowledge and growth of the self: freedom and choice. Together, freedom and choice have given him the opportunity for trial and error, for discovery and exploration. They have enabled him to take charge of his life. Through them he has, we might say, confirmed his own selfness.

Confirmation of his individuality has also come from others, and chiefly from the love and recognition offered to him by the rest of his family. You have let him know that you feel he is of incomparable and immeasurable worth. You have valued his presence and companionship, and you have accepted his unique pattern of physical and mental growth, which is the core of his individuality. You have participated jointly with him in life by being present and available as a source of learning and enrichment.

You are the resource center.
More and more, as he has grown older, you have also become a resource center for him. You have provided toys and games and building and drawing and other creative materials to help expand his perception and develop his skills. Your role and purpose, it is hoped, have been and will continue to be not to manipulate and control your child's interests and development—not to take charge of his *self*—but to make available resources that are based on his own interests and directions and patterns of behavior.

The concept of selfhood is molded at home.
It should be emphasized that your child's concept of self is molded and formed more at home than anywhere else. It cannot be "taught" to your child in school—though some teachers report that parents seem to want to leave it to them to establish a child's self concept and others think they should mold the child, and think they can do so better than the parents can. Your guidance and the atmosphere you create at home will make the strongest contribution to this very basic aspect of your child's development.

Your child's mental growth is a patterning process, and his mind is, therefore, the sum total of an ever-growing mass of patterns of behavior. (A pattern of behavior is any movement or action which has a definite form; it can be as simple as sitting down or grasping an object, or as complicated as riding a bicycle or writing by hand.) These patterns undergo rapid and continuous transformation as your youngster acquires or drops or modifies habits.

Intelligence is dynamic.
Since his mental growth is a patterning process in continuous flux, his intelligence is not fixed, despite opinions to the contrary held until very recently. As the end product of a number of changing factors, it is dynamic. His brain is no longer thought of as a sort of telephone switchboard, capable of certain fixed and static or reflex operations from the time it was created. Rather, it is thought of as an electronic computer. Within it may be stored infinite memories, or information, and patterns of behavior. It is capable of actions which deal with the information, by arranging it in orderly programs, to produce logical operations and, in a word, to solve problems.

The six exclusively human abilities.
Psychologists have found six abilities which are exclusively human and which arise, as neurological functions, from the computerlike intelligence of human beings. Three are motor skills. They are based on the other three, which are sensory skills. The first of the motor skills is the ability to walk

entirely upright. The second is the ability to speak in a symbolic and devised language. The third is the ability to combine manual proficiency with other motor abilities to write the language. The three sensory skills are: the ability to understand the symbolic and devised language that one hears; the ability to identify an object by touch alone; and the ability to see, in a way that enables one to read, the symbolic and devised language when it is in written form.

By the time he is twice as old as he is now, your child will have completely mastered these six exclusively human functions. From then on, if he lives to be twenty-five times as old as he is now, whatever abilities he learns will be but lateral extensions or multiplications of them.

What can you do to help develop the self?

From these rather basic and general psychological points about your five-year-old's development of self, let us move now to the practical and specific things you can do to help him get ready for school within that self. All should come casually, not as drill or test and not on any fixed schedule, but during the course of the day's events—and with heaps of praise for honest effort and jobs well done.

Eyes.

Begin with his awareness of the five senses. While all five are undoubtedly functioning normally, he may not be getting the most out of them. Encourage him to sharpen his sight, to notice that the leaves of different trees have different shapes, that houses vary in size and design, that he can find countless individual differences in things which are generically the same, whether he is discovering the shapes of milk containers or the color of people's eyes and hair and skin or the infinite variety of shoes and hats and neckties. Help him to recognize colors—red, yellow, blue, orange, pink, purple, green, brown, and black—and then to distinguish the subtleties and shades of color, such as bright and dull, reddish and grayish, pale and deep. Find out if he sees what isn't there—a missing part or object. You can assemble buttons, coins, bottletops, anything at all that's around the house, and make a game of "What's missing?" when you take one or two away. You can draw simple stick figures with missing parts to help him see what is absent. Simple puzzles, made by cutting pictures from a magazine, pasting them to a shoe-box top, and cutting it into a puzzle are also an aid.

Ears.

The same question applies to his hearing. Does he notice? You can help him notice by asking him to shut his eyes and listen, anywhere, any time of day, on the spur of the moment. Traffic noises, church bells, workmen hammering or drilling, train whistles, distant radios or television sets playing or pianos being practiced—all should be music to his ears. So should real music, from whatever source. If you have a piano or other instrument around the house, or a fairly good ear yourself, you can try him on listening to the pitch of a note or two or an entire song and then repeating it. Then, to help his ears sharpen their critical listening ability, put to work the casual sound that is immediately at hand. Rice, salt, and cereal each has its own sound when the box is shaken, and a four- to five-year-old with his eyes tightly closed can have a merry guessing game while he listens to them. Try sloshing bottles of salad oil, milk, or juice near his ear while his eyes are closed. A knife tapped on a glass tumbler makes one kind of tinkle, on a teacup another, while a pencil rapped on a table or a ball bounced on the floor have their own sounds. Around the house you will find hundreds more ways to help your child learn about sound.

Nose and tongue.

You get at least three chances every day to help him learn about taste and smell: breakfast, lunch, and dinner. Include him in meal preparations. The taste of cocoa is one thing, and the taste of what pours into the cup is another. Many foods smell and taste differently before and after cooking, and you can let your child smell and taste many of them before and after. Help him to notice other odors, too. Soap and perfumes in the bathroom, disinfectant or antiseptic when he cuts or scrapes himself, a magazine fresh from its wrapper in the mail, gasoline vapors and exhaust at the gas station, shoe polish, and paint. Help him as well to notice different general odors— in supermarkets, libraries, small-town dry-goods or ten-cent stores, drugstores, laundromats, and the like.

Fingers.

Touch, like the other four senses, is used abundantly without conscious reaction; so help your child by drawing attention to the feel of things. Again, guessing games with the eyes closed can be great fun. Assemble objects such as wool and wood, an apple and a peach, metal and plastic. Varieties of cloth alone—gingham and silk, velvet and felt, linen and chintz—can help develop an awareness of the subtleties of feeling. You can go on to various textures of paper and cardboard, of leather, glass, upholstery, carpeting—you name it—including bookbindings and the leaves of potted plants. While you're at it, don't forget that shapes, both inside and outside, are as important as textures. Invite the exploration of the insides of boxes and shoes and pots and pans, and the outsides of keys and tableware, eggs and pears. Sometimes you can combine texture and shape with awareness of change. An unused tea bag has one shape and feel, a used one quite another.

Personal habits of health and dressing help your child to get ready for school. You'd be surprised how many parents are still dressing their children every morning, even after they have started to go to school. They are failing to help motor skills develop, encouraging dependence, and creating extra work for the teacher. Your child should be wearing clothes that he can handle easily himself, and learning to zip zippers, button buttons, lace laces, tie shoes and other bows, hook hooks (and unhook them—an extremely small-muscle operation requiring motion in just the opposite direction from the one any sensible person would expect). He should be able to use the bathroom by himself, as well as the things in it—toothbrush, hairbrush and comb, soap and towel—with satisfactory results.

Large and small muscles.

Indoors and out, you can encourage activities that develop skill in the large muscles. Your child can run and jump, but can he hop on one foot? Can he skip? (Girls can usually skip before boys the same age.) Can he wiggle on the floor like a snake or walk on all fours with back to the floor and tummy to the ceiling like a crab? Climbing, sliding, swinging, coasting in a wagon or on a sled—all call for co-ordination that you can help develop mainly by making it available. Don't forget stairs: many a dweller in ranch house or elevator apartment house has had very little experience with walking up and down steps. Throwing and catching a ball is important—first a large one, then a small one.

Now how about the small muscles? Cutting and pasting are fine exercisers. If your child has never done much cutting, it is a good idea to begin by drawing simple shapes yourself. Then let him draw his own, and next he may graduate to cutting pictures from magazines. He can make his own paste from flour and water. Crayons and plenty of cheap blank paper (a ream of the least expensive mimeograph paper in the stationery store is one of the best sources) should always be on hand. Clay or plastic modeling dough and poster paints are equally important.

Let collecting lead to counting.

The exercise of small-muscle control or skills is combined with the exercise of the senses, noticing what one sees and feels. You can help your child to know and recognize shapes by having him find, cut out, and paste items that are square and round and triangular and by encouraging him to draw such shapes. The game will be enhanced if he finds and "collects" similar shapes in things around the house—a clock, a door frame, a picture, a book. The last will lead him to three-dimensionality, and he can have a marvelous time finding circles and squares that go in more than one direction—a ball, an orange, a box, a can. When such concepts have become second nature to him, try rolling his tricycle onto an opened newspaper and drawing with dark crayon a line between the three points where the wheels touch the paper; or, better yet, let him discover this abstract triangle by drawing it himself.

Cutting and pasting can also lead to an understanding of sets and counting. While chopping up old magazines, let your child make a game of finding things that are alike or belong to the same set. Anything will do—pictures of boys or girls, of cars or trucks or hats or chairs. Have him paste all those that belong together on the same sheet, and help him learn to count them slowly, over and over. (Not more than five on a sheet, though. Counting sets of five is enough for now.) Then let him begin to collect other things to count—preferably, at first, things that belong to the same set, such as beads or pieces of dry macaroni or buttons or pennies. Next, you can show him that things not of the same set may be mingled and counted.

Learning to count is a highly abstract art and achievement. If you begin this way—with sets of physical objects that, for one reason or another, belong together—you will implant an idea of mathematics that is far deeper and more basic than the old rattling off of counting one to ten or one to one hundred by rote. Soon your child will be bouncing around the house inventing games of counting things that are blue or things that are round or things that are light in weight or big or dark or alive.

When you have come this far, set aside the face cards from a pack of old playing cards. Line up one suit in a row from one to ten, and let your youngster make a game of lining up the other three suits to match. You can help him discover how the sets are grouped on each card and how the number is printed in the corner. You might add last month's calendar to the scene, to show the numbers in order.

It's no fun if it becomes work.

Newspaper headlines provide big, simple words to cut out, too, and the cut-and-paste game may be extended to matching letters and words. The ambitious may even begin to trace or copy numbers and letters with crayon on blank paper. But caution: There is no shame in not being able to go this far, and there is no fun if it becomes work. Don't ever give the impression that any of this *has* to be done.

Don't hesitate to use fingers and toes for counting. Probably you counted toes long ago, with "This little pig went to market." And if you have used the calendar to show him printed numbers, it will be equally useful in helping him understand the date of his birthday. To teach him his age, try drawing a set of four birthday cakes, with candles from one to four. You will give him an idea more memorable and understandable than mere rote memorizing of the word "four."

You'd be surprised at how many children arrive at kindergarten without having learned any of these abilities—or motor-sensory skills—at home. Some schools have found it necessary to set up special motor-sensory programs, using parent volunteers to help bring the Johnny-come-latelies up to the skills of their peers.

Answer those questions.

A sense of wonder is developing, and questions will be opening up faster and faster now. It is important to let your child know that he can talk to you about anything and that you are really interested in what he is saying. Whatever he comes up with, try to give him an answer. If you don't have the answer, say so frankly and then help him find the answer. Don't hesitate to ask him questions, too. He learns to think by thinking, and he is open to all kinds of ideas.

Eating and sleeping habits should be set now, too, in preparation for the pattern of going to school. Ten to twelve hours of sleep, with a regular bedtime and regular rising time, are needed. Meals should come at regular hours and with enough time so that good food and good company may be enjoyed. Your four- to five-year-old knows best how much food he needs at any one time, but he does not know what foods are best for him. It is easier to get him to sample a bite or two of an unknown food if a favorite is on the plate with it. Getting hungry between meals is quite legitimate, and so is a nourishing snack. An occasional candy bar is not poison. What is important is what is learned and associated with eating: that food itself is pleasant to see and taste and smell, that it may be served in a variety of ways and in many places, and that mealtime is a happy time.

If your five-year-old never gets angry or loses his temper, there is something wrong. Interference with his physical activities is especially apt to cause an outburst. However, by this age he is probably surprising you at times with his ability to control his anger. The concepts of fair play and sharing, of "please" and "thank you," of keeping his word, and of trusting you and other authorities will be easily embraced if he learns that they do bring pleasant results.

There is a difference between self and selfishness. If your youngster can do no wrong, if the whole family and its activities revolve around keeping him happy, he is going to pay heavily in the classroom. His self-centered attitude will probably stir up trouble with his schoolmates, and it will make demands on the teacher which she will not have time to fulfill. Of course, if you have been spoiling your child for three or four years and you stop suddenly now just when he is about to go to school, you are in for some rough times. But the sooner you begin de-spoiling, the better.

Use the household social systems.

The kindergarten is a social system and it is the second social system your child will learn. The first, which he has already learned, is the family. In fact, your household is a sort of cultural workshop in which all aspects of the self which have been discussed have been developing.

Daily jobs and duties are valuable to your developing child. You do many jobs in order to take care of him, and at times one of his jobs is to keep out of your way. But there are other jobs he can do—take care of his clothing and possessions, put away toys and work materials, toss dirty clothes into the laundry hamper and neatly put clean things in his chest of drawers. Bed making may be an ambitious job, but a lumpy bed made by him has more long-term value than a smooth one made by you. Dishwashing, dusting, taking out the garbage, feeding pets, watering plants, setting the table—all appeal to his natural desire to be helpful. An important thing to remember about all jobs at this age is that they are fun to do if other members of the family are around at the time. They prepare the way for the many setting-up, cleaning-up, and errand-running jobs to come in school.

Establish some house rules.

Some general "house rules" about orderliness and co-operation with other members of the family are the best foundation for the rules that will come in school. Most likely, such rules will be implicit in day-to-day jobs, duties, and relationships rather than explicitly stated, since preaching and laying down the law have never worked in any social system so well as example and leadership. Sharing ideas but waiting, without interrupting, for a chance to speak; sharing games and toys and waiting for a chance to play; telling the truth and knowing that it will be told by others; respecting the property of others as well as his own and expecting others to respect his; being considered in family plans that concern him and finding his suggestions and ideas for family plans accepted and respected—all are house rules that will apply in the classroom as well.

What about watching television? Two basic results of his watching can be stated. If your child has watched as much as the average American child, he now has a larger vocabulary, a wider frame of reference, and a larger store of general information than the rare child who has been deprived of this opportunity.

Make TV viewing selective.

Two things should be remembered about television. One is that you and your child *together* can be selective. Watch what he watches now and then, and talk with him about it; his judgments on the value of what he sees may surprise you. Talk about what he is going to see; plans can be made for the use of the TV set, and they can be stuck to. The second thing to notice is that distraction from TV is easy. If something more interesting is offered or is going on, few children *or* grownups will stick to TV.

One effective distraction is a good book and a parent who is willing to read it aloud, for no amount of TV involvement has yet replaced the joyous "play" of hearing stories read and seeing pictures turned by a close member of the family. It makes familiar the printed medium that is fairly sure to be the chief learning source through the seventeen or more years of your offspring's formal education.

Know the effect of television on your child. If he is heavily addicted to the tube, he is living in a world of rhetoric. It is not a real world. He needs a world of the senses—of play with neighborhood children or, if his immediate world lacks peers, of more organized play in nursery school or play group. The point is for him to interact with other human beings—not with images on the screen.

How important is "Sesame Street"? Opinions vary. Some principals say that the program's impact on the language experience of children has been highly overrated. Some teachers say the program has an undeniable influence in helping children to recognize letter shapes earlier but note that the novelty appears to have worn off. One says, "Books from 'Sesame Street' aren't grabbed up in the library the way they used to be." Another says, "It's difficult for a teacher to compete today with Big Bird. Teachers must work with it, rather than against. Children who have not been allowed to view 'Sesame Street' usually are lost and struggle to get the concepts that others have already grasped." Still another says, " 'Sesame Street' delivers little more than entertainment unless parents assist children in activating the concepts presented."

In many school districts, getting ready for school within the home is highlighted by a visit from the kindergarten teacher. Some come to the home as early as the spring or summer before school begins, while others come around during the first two or three weeks of school in September. Such visits help tremendously in bridging the gap between home and school. Your child sees the teacher as a welcome guest in his own home, and the teacher gets a chance to give him undivided attention while he shows off his pets, toys, and games, his room and home. You, on the other hand, get a chance to fill the teacher in on any existing health problems and to talk about the interests, experiences, and fears of the child whom she wants to know and whom you know so well.

Getting ready away from home.

Equally important as preparation within the home is the opportunity of taking the future pupil to see the school. Your school may issue a special invitation during the spring or summer. There may be an open house on registration day, giving your child a tour of the school building and introducing you not only to the teacher but to the principal, the nurse, and other staff members.

When you go to visit the school, take the route your child will be taking. Let the streets and neighborhoods along the way become familiar beforehand. Remember that the building may look very large and frightening to his eyes, and that one class of children, seen in action on the playground, may look to him like a mob—especially when all are strangers. You can make the point that it takes a big building to hold all the children who come to school to learn and that he will soon make friends with many of them and know their names.

Go anywhere and everywhere.

You can do far more than take him to see his future school. It is a fact of his development that the more new things he has seen and the more he has heard, the more things he is interested in seeing and hearing. The greater the variety of situations to which he must accommodate or adapt his behavior, the more adaptable that behavior becomes. So take him anywhere and everywhere: on a picnic in city park or country woodland; to zoo and circus; to whatever stores, large or small, you shop in (a preschooler left in a car in a parking lot is a preschooler missing a valuable learning experience); to a beach and to a farm; on elevator and escalator; and in bus, boat, train and airplane. The library is an important stop, but so is the drugstore or the delicatessen.

Explain how things work. See if your child knows where the stock boys get the cans they are loading onto supermarket shelves, who will take away the letter he drops into the mailbox for you, what the cobbler will do with the shoes you leave behind, why the on-the-premises cleaner's shop is always so hot and steamy.

See whole worlds.

Help him gain a sense of a whole world. A museum is one kind of whole world, a world of collections and exhibits and samples of life and experience that are not ready to hand. A farm is another kind of whole world. Still another world may be seen in a small town, where you can point out post office and bank, gas station and grocery store, school and church, and establish the idea of the community. In a city you can expand that idea, by showing the world of various neighborhoods—business and shopping, industrial and residential. Then there are national parks, with the world of nature preserved and protected, and seashore areas, with the world of nature and recreation and commerce combined.

On all such trips, whether a five-minute shopping errand downtown or a three-week vacation tour, don't forget that all five of your child's senses have come along with him. Whether he is perceiving like mad or just going along for the ride may depend on how much fun you make it by helping to call his attention to the sights, sounds, odors, taste, and feel of all that he encounters. Not that you can or should make it a constant practice to nudge your child's awareness, or that circumstances will always permit you to. Dr. Montessori learned more than sixty years ago to endure the displeasure of museum guards who were shocked when tour groups from her school came in and "touched everything." Even today it is a rare museum or display that permits children to sense the three-dimensionality of an object with anything but their eyes.

Get a well-baby checkup.

One necessary trip before school opens is to see a doctor for a checkup. Probably your school will send you a form for the doctor to fill out. In most states, immunization against smallpox, diphtheria, tetanus, measles, German measles (rubella), mumps, whooping cough, and polio are required. Chances are your child has already had the necessary injections, but if shots or boosters are needed, be sure to help him understand that everybody gets them and that they help keep sickness from spreading. With 95 out of 100 kids, the preschool trip to the doctor is nothing more than what the medics call a "well-baby checkup."

No examination by the school doctor or nurse can take the place of a thorough checkup by your doctor. The checkup should come in plenty of time before September, preferably in the spring, so that you have time to start treatment if any should be needed.

A visit to the eye specialist and a dental cleaning and checkup are wise, too, subject to the advice your pediatrician or family doctor gives you. Such checkups, by doctor, dentist, and eye specialist, can help keep such problems as major cavities or abscessed teeth, impaired hearing, or poor vision from interfering with school life.

If it can be managed, it's a good idea to make several trips before school begins to places away from home where you can leave your child for a short time. Visiting an aunt or uncle or good friend helps loosen his grip on the apron strings and gives him the idea that away from home is sometimes a good place to be, that he can be there and have happy times without you, and that he can and will go home again.

What about nursery school and Head Start?

What about a more formal, organized, and regularly scheduled form of getting ready for school? There are several such opportunities available, ranging from expensive nursery schools to Project Head Start and day-care centers.

Want to try a play group?

You might get involved in a play group. This is usually a very small group (not more than half a dozen) of three- and four-year-olds who meet regularly at one another's homes to play. Each mother in turn supervises the entire group. The play group is not thought of as a baby-sitting arrangement, but has a planned and prepared program. It uses materials and equipment supplied by the group and introduced by the mother in charge. In effect, the play group operates in an area usually reserved for professionals and depends on informed mothers to maintain its semiprofessionalism. Its main importance is that it offers your child a chance to be with other children. Probably the only cost will be your share of the materials, since you and the other mothers will contribute your time and a place to meet.

The idea behind the play group is the fact that even though preschool children do not play together as they will in another year or so, their play takes on a different meaning when they are together. They learn to share toys and art materials and to get to know and share other mothers than their own. They begin to get the feeling of belonging to a group, and at the same time they begin to develop self-confidence and independence. They have fun, too.

Of course, the play group also benefits you. It will give you free time when your child goes to another house, and it will give you insight when the group comes to your house.

Does nursery school lead to Harvard? To MIT?

Nationwide, it has been estimated that about two million children attend nursery school. This is well over half of the four-year-old population. In such affluent communities as Pound Ridge, New York, or the Point Loma section of San Diego, the nursery-school experience among kindergartners runs as high as 98 per cent, with the majority having had two full years. The first half of the 1970's saw nursery-school attendance increase dramatically—by about 60 per cent—although attendance dropped by about 13 per cent in 1977.

No one knows exactly how many children are sent to nursery school because their parents think it is the launching pad for a trip to Harvard or MIT. There are other more valid reasons. One-third of the mothers of preschool children are in the labor force, working regularly. Two out of five children currently live in single-parent families for at least part of their childhoods; so they are likely candidates for nursery school. And children today have fewer brothers and sisters to mix with and learn from—the "statistically average child" has less than one sibling, whereas a generation ago the average child had almost three.

What are the advantages of nursery school for three- and four-year-olds? They adjust more easily to the school situation. Their social skills are better developed. Depending on the nursery school's standards, they have had some exposure to "readiness"—an exposure that may come also from play school or from home.

The male teacher.

In some nursery schools, one finds an advantage almost never found in public kindergarten: the male teacher. Men in the nursery are especially welcome to children who live only with their mothers or whose fathers are frequently absent on business. At least one nursery school, in Sherman Oaks, California, has three males to one female teacher. A parent notes that the men there seem less concerned about structure and regimentation and are more creative than women with the materials they use. Male nursery teachers also help overcome—or at least delay—establishing in the youngsters' minds the stereotype that caring for children is women's work.

The popularity of nursery school is creating some problems of logistics and curriculum in kindergarten. Nursery schools usually run about three hours a day (some, however, run from early morning to late afternoon to accommodate working parents). Public kindergarten in most communities runs only two-and-a-half hours, because the teacher must handle two complete sessions each day, one in the morning and one in the afternoon.

All-day Kindergarten.

Under public pressure, the law has changed in some communities to make all-day kindergarten compulsory. However, because five-year-olds tire whether or not the law makes them go to school all day, effective teaching can go on for only two-and-a-half or three hours. The rest of the time, kindergarten becomes a day-care center, with naps, snacks, and play. One solution you may see evolving is this: Elementary schools may develop a program in which the kindergarten teacher handles only one group each day, in the morning. In a three-hour session, the developmental activities are pursued—listening, music, concepts, physical activities. In the afternoon, the teacher resumes with those who need special attention, review, or remedial work; the others have gone home. As one principal puts it, "This would put us ahead of any movement that equates more time for children in kindergarten with 'academic excellence'—the 'in' phrase at the moment—but it would be more expensive because the kindergarten teacher would handle only one session a day."

Variations in quality.

Nursery schools vary in quality, and their value is directly proportional to the skill and background of the teacher. You may find near you a nursery school sponsored by a major university either through its education department or its departments of child psychology or child development. Or you may find in your neighborhood a nursery school set up by a young mother who majored in primary education and who is interested in running her school for a few years in order to enhance the experience of her own children. Between these two extremes, you will find many private or cooperative nursery schools which are well established in their communities. Any of these offers the advantages of sharing, being together in a group, adjusting to authority other than the parent, developing self-confidence and independence. While nursery school does provide these advantages, it leads to what some school principals observe as a common assumption among parents that their children are getting a cognitive program and will later find kindergarten boring.

Watch out for promises.

One expert, Dr. Burton White, senior research associate at the Harvard School of Education and author of *The First Three Years of Life,* has warned against nursery schools that promise to be "educationally powerful." Says White: "If a school makes claim to that, it doesn't know what it's talking about. A certain educational method might provide entertainment, socializing or short-term learning impact, but none of the so-called revolutionary teaching techniques has demonstrated that it can provide anything educationally significant to a child from a good home."

More than one annual survey has found that mothers believe that nursery school provides their children with an opportunity to relate to other children the same age but that fathers believe nursery school exists to give the mothers a break. The nursery school is, in fact, a middle-class phenomenon in America, and experts such as psychologists, pediatricians, and sociologists, who are not directly involved in early childhood education but who are related to the field and have clear views of it, express a wide range of opinions on nursery school. Some say that the curriculum is too stereotyped, that the nursery-school field tries to be all things to all people, and that there are no standards to judge the value of specific nursery schools. Others approve the very fact that there is a variety of motivations for sending children to nursery school, and say that the curriculum is a truly liberal-arts offering and that the "traditional" nursery school does a fine job.

Even though the range is wide, it is important to remember, when you consider nursery school, that you are considering a field of education in which, with very few exceptions, teachers and schools are not certified or regulated. Therefore you must look closely and exercise your own judgment. An example of one thing to avoid is the nursery school that belongs to the "approval culture." One little boy who attended such a school came home each day and told his father that he had made a finger painting that day and that the teacher said it was very good. After two weeks of finger painting and daily approval, he brought home his latest "very good" painting, showed it to his father, and said, "How do you make a *bad* finger painting?" He was ready, like most children of three or older, to assess his own efforts. He did not need continual approval in order to feel good. He was the victim of the general theory that only his emotional and social growth, not his mental growth, can be influenced in nursery school.

Head Start quality varies.

In many communities, both urban and rural, you will find public-school programs for prekindergartners. A pioneer was Baltimore's Early Admissions Program, which began in 1963. Project Head Start was launched in 1965, financed by antipoverty funds from the United States Office of Economic Opportunity. Originally, it was a summer program to give preschool children from deprived backgrounds a head start on going to school. The program soon moved to a year-round basis, and has become a fixture in school districts where the cost of private nursery schools would be out of the question for the majority of parents. Example: In affluent Fairfield County, Connecticut, the alumni of Head Start are in the majority in kindergarten in blue-collar Norwalk, while in neighboring white-collar New Canaan not a single kindergartner (more than 90 per cent of whom have had nursery-school experience) has ever seen a Head Start classroom.

Like so many things, Head Start quality varies. A large, rural, regional school in western New York State reported in 1978, "Our program here is excellent now—strong and a real benefit to both underprivileged and culturally deprived." Yet a major urban school in the State of Washington said in the same year, "The instructional program of Head Start remains inappropriate to the needs of the undereducated population it serves, modeling still after preschools for more advantaged pupils. When Head Start pupils reach kindergarten, it is difficult to tell that they have a prior learning experience."

Milwaukee's extensive program.

Some school systems have developed a growing number of preschool classes for three- and four-year-olds. The Milwaukee public schools offer not only Head Start (described there as an "interdisciplinary approach to total school readiness for low income preschool children and families") but well over a dozen distinct and separate programs. Examples include:

□ Cooperative Play: the development of skills, habits, patterns of learning through play and recreational activities.

□ LEAP (Learning Early to Achieve Potential): helping child to achieve potential; strengthening parents' skills as educators of their children.

□ Title III—ESEA Multi-Media Home Education Project: development of parenting skills through direct, radio, and television instruction; refinement of children's listening skills through radio instruction.

□ Four-Year-Old Kindergarten: Some half-dozen options range from parent education through home visits by teachers, individual conferences, and group meetings to family education in Montessori philosophy, observation, and preparation of materials.

□ Title I—ESEA Preschool Project Center Home Program: School readiness for educationally needful children in their homes, in established centers, and in self-contained classrooms.

One final thought about preschool programs: The most important preschool program of all is the one you conduct informally and continuously in an entirely unstructured way at home. Culturally deprived four-year-olds may not speak in sentences, but teachers can also tell you about many a kindergartner from a middle-income family who has come to school unable to put words into sentences simply because he has been talked *at* a great deal but talked *with* and listened to very little. For reasons different from those of the culturally deprived, he has had no exercise in conversation.

4

Going to School

When do you register your child? How does he get to school? What if he begs to take along a favorite doll or teddy bear? Should you send crayons or other supplies? If the school needs to reach you when you're not at home, what do they do? A hundred nagging questions may occur to you as September draws near.

When to register.

Most schools have at least two registration periods—one in the spring and another a week or two before school opens in September. Your local newspaper is sure to carry announcements of the dates. As mentioned earlier, there is usually an open house on registration day so that you can tour the school and meet teachers and staff.

What to take.

You will need proof of your child's age. His birth certificate is expected, but in unusual cases some schools will accept a baptismal certificate or even a passport. Certificates or statements of immunization signed by your doctor will be required, and you will be asked to fill in a form listing parent's place of employment and the telephone number of a neighbor or relative, so that someone may be called if you don't answer at home when illness or emergency arises.

You will be asked what name your child is to be called by. Some teachers avoid using nicknames, though most like to call a child by the name he is used to. Some parents want their child to answer to a middle name, and every once in a while there comes a boy or girl who has been brought up to answer to a name not found anywhere on the official records. Susan Phelps Smith, says her mother, *must* be called "Meredith." Nothing else will do. If your child is to be known by something other than his given first name, the time to say so is when you register him.

A 'screening' is not a 'test'.

In some schools, you may be asked some simple and basic questions about your family group and your child's experience. These are intended to guide the teacher and school principal in understanding your child. Your child may also be screened to help establish his stage of development. The purpose is to find out what level of social, intellectual and physical maturity your child has reached. Some schools put more mature kindergartners together in the afternoon class, less mature in the morning, so the teacher can work more closely with each. Such grouping, by the way, has its greatest value early in the school year; by June, as the teacher has worked to meet the needs of each, the groups will just about match in maturity levels.

Parent questionnaires and screening interviews for kindergartners are not compulsory. While their purpose is to give the school people information on how the parents perceive their youngsters, occasionally some parents object. Most schools today respect the parents' right to privacy and will not insist on your answering any questions that you prefer not to answer. Typical questionnaires and screening instruments are shown in Appendix A.

Practice going to school.

If the school is within walking distance, it is a good idea to practice walking there with your child at precisely the times he will be going and coming. The traffic at eight forty-five in the morning is likely to be quite different from that at eleven or at two in the afternoon. Whether he is going to walk alone or with an escort, teach him pedestrian rules and habits: to take the shortest route; to walk on the sidewalk if there is one, or on the left side of the road so that he faces oncoming traffic; to cross the street only at corners and never from between parked cars; to look in all possible traffic directions before crossing and then to walk, not run; to understand and obey traffic lights and the signals of policemen and crossing guards; and never to walk on railroad tracks or through parking lots or loading areas.

Riding the school bus.

If a school bus is provided, a letter from the school or a listing in your newspaper will tell you the time and place your child will be picked up. If he goes to the morning session of kindergarten, he will ride to school with older children but come home on a special bus. If he's an afternooner, he will go on a special bus and come home with the regular all-age crowd.

Probably you have seen school-bus stops where the waiting children look like a bunch of Mexican jumping beans. It is next to impossible to stop the activity, but your supervision at the bus stop may help you move it back from the edge of a busy highway. School-bus manners will be helped if you have talked over with your child the need for boarding and leaving the bus in an orderly fashion, for listening to the driver's instructions, and for being considerate of the other kids who are aboard.

In some schools, bus drivers are instructed to return to the school any kindergarten child whose parent or parent representative does not meet him at the bus stop. All schools enforce the rule that no child may ride a bus other than his regular one unless a note has come from home that day. So if your child plans to go to someone else's house to play after school, make sure he has written permission to ride someone else's bus. Once in a while someone does get aboard the wrong bus. Most drivers are instructed to make a special trip to such a pupil's appointed stop after they complete their regular route.

Bus drivers hold their buses with warning lights flashing until all children have safely crossed the street in front of the bus. You can help by teaching your child to step around far enough in front of the bus so that he can be seen by the driver, and by teaching him not to depend on the flashing lights to stop traffic. He might as well learn now that there is always some idiot who can't be bothered with the rules and that he must look both ways to make sure that idiot has not invaded his neighborhood.

Warnings: strangers and weather.

Whether walking to school, waiting at a bus stop, or walking between the bus stop and home, your child may be offered a ride. It is hoped that before now you have taught him never to ride with strangers.

A word about weather. Rain and snow mean starting earlier because going will be slower, and they mean being more alert to possible dangers. Cars need longer distances to stop, and bad weather cuts down visibility. One of the chief problems with pedestrians of any age is to get them to see themselves from the point of view of the person behind the wheel. Try to get your youngster to understand that he has to do a lot of watching himself because he just may not be seen.

Things to take to school.

Different schools make different requests about what to bring. Yours may ask each child to bring a pair of sneakers and a cloth bag to keep them in. It will probably want a work apron or smock or one of Dad's old shirts. For the brief midday rest period, a small bath mat or towel or rag rug may be required. One side should be marked with tape or colored thread so that it can always be turned "up" from the floor. In some states and cities, you will be asked to supply crayons and paste, scissors and art paper. But don't load your child with all these things the very first day. The school will send a note asking for them when they are wanted. The school will tell you when to send milk money. When you send it, send the exact amount.

No one can overstress the importance of marking names on clothing. School lost-and-found closets contain incredible collections of hats, scarves, mittens, overshoes, and sweaters. And loops on things that are to be hung up—coats, sweaters, snow pants—will help your child keep order in his cubby.

The day when children were forbidden to bring things from home seems to be past. Teachers recognize the value of a favorite toy or stuffed animal or doll being lugged to school both as a companion and as something to show. But it will help if you remind your child that his classmates will probably want to see and share his favorite possession. You both must realize that the school cannot be responsible for its safe conduct. If the possession is fragile or irreplaceable, it is better off at home.

Part Two

The Day in School

Before opening day, your child's teacher will have made a name tag for him to wear, which will show his full name and address, his teacher's name, and, if appropriate, his school-bus number. She will have made another tag for his locker or cubby, and perhaps she will have made him a paper hat with his name on it. She will also have arranged the various activity areas to fit in with her plans for conducting the class.

The daily program that she plans must be flexible enough to accommodate occasional changes imposed by emergencies and special events—such as fire drills and auditorium programs and field trips. Certain things must be done each day at scheduled times, establishing a regular and consistent sequence of activities so that pupils gain a sense of security. The program, which must balance alternate periods of activity and rest, calls for considerable variety to meet the needs of the pupils' different capacities and to provide them with varied and interesting materials. It must be divided into blocks of time long enough to accomplish its objectives but short enough not to overtire nor to exceed rather short attention spans, especially early in the year.

The first day.

Some first-day sessions welcome the entire kindergarten class at once, while others organize the newcomers into small groups for short lengths of time. If your school is receiving the entire class during the ten-minute period when the school buses unload, your child's teacher probably has one or two helpers who are experienced mothers from last year's kindergarten. Many schools, however, in the hope of making the adjustment to school as gentle as possible, use some kind of gradual entrance plan. In some, during the first week or so, two shortened sessions are held, with half of the class attending each session. In others, only ten children are told to come for the entire session the first day, with another five joining them the second day, five more the third day, and so on until the entire class attends full time.

Such gradual entrance plans give both the teacher and the children a chance to get to know one another at once. The children, starting off in a small group, become acquainted a few at a time. They feel close to the teacher from the beginning, and the confusion and fear of the unknown that come from entering a crowded atmosphere are lessened. First, they find out about the room, then the playground, then the building and other school personnel so that they will become secure in each physical environment.

No matter how many or how few pupils come to class together, it is just about impossible for the teacher to use the regular schedule on the first day. Welcoming them, showing them where to put their belongings and where to find work and play materials—everything takes longer than it will take only a day or two later. Cleaning-up routines cannot be established at once, nor milk money collected, nor rest periods established. It is important for you to discuss these aspects of the first day or two with your child and to help him understand that all the boys and girls he sees in his schoolroom are starting from the beginning as he is.

The typical day.

In looking at the daily program it's better not to think of what will happen the very first day—though much of it *may* happen the first day—but of what will happen most days as soon as the school year gets rolling.

This section of the book is designed to give you and your child an idea of the structure of the typical kindergarten day, whether in morning or afternoon session. Naturally, no two schools are exactly alike, and details are certain to vary. However, the general patterns and routines are the same in schools in city or country, north or south, east or west.

ARRIVAL: FREE PLAY

What happens: Your child plays with blocks, puzzles, construction toys, felt board, alphabet cutouts, dolls, paints, or any other materials and games available in the room.

Why it happens: While we call it play, psychologists and teachers of teachers call it "structuring reality." Whichever you prefer to call it, this activity period has real purpose and meaning. It settles your child into the classroom atmosphere, enables him to translate his knowledge, feelings, and fantasies into action, and gives him a natural approach to understanding life situations. Daily, it exercises his skills in problem solving and in motor control, expands his use of language and his social adaptability, and encourages his autonomy.

Time: Twenty to 30 minutes. (Note: During the free-play period, as during each activity throughout the school day, your child's teacher will maintain an over-all "feel" for the situation, extending the time of the activity if it seems to be going profitably for all and shortening it if she notices restlessness and boredom.)

CLEANUP TIME

What happens: All materials in use are cleaned up and put away by the children under the teacher's direction.

Why it happens: Apart from getting the room ready for the next activity, it is important to develop a sense of responsibility for the room and a feeling of pride in its appearance. Your child is encouraged to feel competent in caring for the materials he uses. Helpfulness is encouraged. Those who were doing something that is quickly and easily cleaned up are welcome to help those who have more pieces to pick up or more mess to clean.

Time: Approximately five minutes. (Note: Cleanup is repeated later after the work period and again whenever conditions demand.)

OPENING EXERCISES

What happens: Salute to the flag. Attendance. Calendar discussion.

Why it happens: Though the emotional value of the ritual may reach your child before he comprehends its patriotic value, he learns to recognize the flag as a symbol of our country and its people. He practices listening and repeating as he recites the difficult words of the pledge of allegiance. If he is one of those who have not yet learned to differentiate between left and right, he is helped by daily putting his right hand over his heart.

In taking attendance, the teacher often asks the boys to count the girls and vice versa, or she plays a "Who's missing?" game. She thus finds out who can count and who is observant, and the class exercises counting and language and deductive skills.

Talk of weather and of special days (such as Ground Hog Day or the birthday of either a famous person or a member of the class) encourages conversation and the sharing of ideas, and it develops awareness of days of the week, of numerical symbols for days of the month, and of seasonal aspects of the month and the time of the year.

Time: Approximately five minutes.

THE WORK PERIOD

What happens: Individuals, small groups, or the entire class work with manipulative materials such as clay, poster paint, finger paint, or thicker paint which involves the use of sponge, feathers, scrub brush, or potato ends as printers. Other materials are chalk or crayons. Collages are made from scraps and yarn, seeds and shells, and so on. Construction includes paper sculpture, use of the workbench, and woodworking, as well as playing with blocks, plastic bricks, and metal assemblies. Housekeeping includes dramatic play in the doll corner and with toy utensils. Science "finding-out" work uses magnifying glass, magnets, scales, levers, old clocks, and latches. Plants are grown for nature study. Pegs, beads, cubes, dominoes, and puzzles are matched for color, shape, number, and design.

Why it happens: While the earlier free-play period was "for the fun of it," the work period sets a task and a goal. Your child learns how to use and manipulate the various materials, to work with a purpose and to want to improve and finish what he has started, to solve problems and experiment with new ideas and think before acting, to follow directions and find interesting ways to supplement them, to work with others courteously and thoughtfully and quietly. The work period helps him to understand and interpret the world around him and acquaints him with a variety of activities that help him develop physically, mentally, socially, emotionally, and aesthetically. It gives him a chance to work independently at his own pace on activities that he has planned and chosen and helps him also to learn to share ideas and materials while he co-operates with his classmates in group activities.

Time: Half an hour early in the year, extending to 40 or 45 minutes later.

TOILET AND WASHING

What happens: Most primary-school facilities are scaled to size, and your child is encouraged to be independent about using them.

Why it happens: The facilities of the room and the building dictate how the washing up and the use of the toilet are organized. If the washrooms are somewhere down the hall, a regular washroom period and a certain amount of lining up and taking turns may be necessary. If the room has its own washrooms, the children are encouraged to excuse themselves to use the toilet whenever necessary during the day, and they may wash up in the washroom or at the sink in the classroom as soon as they have put away their work.

Time: As needed.

LIBRARY TIME

What happens: The entire class or small groups go to the school library. The librarian sometimes reads to them. They select books to take out and return borrowed books.

Why it happens: Your child learns the system of borrowing and returning books. He is encouraged to browse, to select, and to "read." He meets authorities other than his teacher: the librarian and one or two volunteer helpers who will see that he finds books that really appeal to his interests.

Time: Approximately fifteen minutes, usually once or twice a week.

READINESS ACTIVITIES

What happens: "Show and tell." Active counting, listening, and memory games. Dramatic play. Passive listening during story time. (Readiness is that stage in your child's physical, mental, emotional, social, and empirical development when he is able to undertake a given learning experience with ease, understanding, and interest.)

Why it happens: Readiness activities (if you will forgive the seeming doubletalk) get ready for readiness. They develop speaking skills, listening skills, prereading skills, number concepts, and motor control and co-ordination. In "show and tell," a child shows the class or a group of children something brought from home or made in school and tells them about it. The purpose is not to force the child into public speaking or embarrassment, but to encourage him to feel at ease when the attention of all is turned on him, as it will be when he responds in more formal class situations in future years. It works two ways, for while your child is showing and telling, the rest of the class is looking and listening.

Time: Fifteen to 30 minutes. (Note: Many of the readiness activities occur informally, either as part of or between other activities. The entire day is, in a sense, devoted to them.)

SNACK AND REST

What happens: Milk and cookies or crackers for all are distributed by the children. Cleanup by the children is followed by a short rest period.

Why it happens: Because five-year-old appetites know, like Pooh, that it is time for a little something. Counting out straws, napkins, milk cartons, and cookies at tables of five or ten helps develop number concepts. Good manners, turn taking, and patience are encouraged as those who have finished must hold up a hand and be recognized before they take napkin and carton to the trash can.

Alternate periods of activity and rest are a fundamental need of all ages, but they are especially important when muscular activity and mental concentration are combined. Emotional control, ability to pay attention, and general behavior improve with a few minutes' rest in school.

The majority of today's kindergartens ask each child to bring a towel or mat for the rest period, and the entire class stretches out on the floor. However, some kindergartens have done away with the rest period. They find that well-spaced quiet times and passive activities serve the purpose just as well. In some schools, on the other hand, small cots are provided. Where the rest period does invite the kindergartner to lie down on cot or rug or mat, he often falls sound asleep.

Time: Ten to fifteen minutes.

MUSIC

What happens: Music is experienced and enjoyed in many situations and contexts throughout the day, often without drawing a line between listening, performing, and creating music. Informal singing, group singing, rhythm and melody instruments, parades, handclapping, finger snapping, toe tapping, dramatizing songs, and running, skipping, and sliding to music are typical of musical activities.

Why it happens: The first and foremost purpose of musical activities is to develop in your child a love of music of all kinds. In addition, music work develops his ear and his ability to carry a tune, teaches him to be comfortable in group singing and to participate in rhythmic movements, encourages him to listen with appreciation to music, strengthens his large muscles and develops his co-ordination in interpreting music, and encourages him to listen attentively and to respond freely, using all parts of his body in expressing a mood or idea as the music is fast or slow, heavy or light, its beat steady or accented.

Time: Twenty to 30 minutes, plus occasional spontaneous singing or rhythmic activity during other periods.

STRENUOUS PLAY

What happens: Indoors: folk and interpretive dancing, games of tag, beanbag tossing, rolling, catching, and bouncing a ball.

Outdoors: monkey bars or jungle gym, slide, seesaw, swings, sandbox, balance board, or log.

Why it happens: Highly organized games, races, and tests of skill require emotional control beyond most kindergartners' ability. However, strenuous play in the kindergarten does mean that all aspects of running, jumping, sliding, hopping, skipping, throwing, catching, and tagging are exercised and developed. The teacher also watches for the exercise of such social skills as fair play and turn taking.

Time: Fifteen to 30 minutes.

DISMISSAL

What happens: Your child goes home—by bus or automobile or on foot—in a well-systematized way. In most parts of the United States and in most seasons, he puts on at least a sweater, and in some places and seasons he wears overshoes and coats and pants that must be buttoned and zipped, plus hat, scarf, and mittens. Occasionally, he carries home some example of his schoolwork, a book from the library, or a note from the teacher—early in the fall any such note is probably pinned to his clothing.

Why it happens: Though help is given where needed, independence and agility in dressing are encouraged. Routines are established in the habits of always boarding school bus or automobile at the same place or always taking the same pedestrian route home.

Time: Up to 15 minutes, depending on the season of the year and the amount of outdoor clothing to be put on.

HOME AGAIN

It probably will do you no good to ask what happened in school today. Children in primary school seem to be universally unresponsive to this classic query from their parents. However, if you are patient, the news will out. Listening to your child and conversing with him about school without grilling him will be important continuing activities for you during this and every school year, and in Part Four we will discuss in greater detail your continuing help at home.

It helps to remember that your kindergartner has packed a great deal of activity and learning experience into the two-and-a-half or three hours he has spent away from you. He is likely to come home pleasantly tired and at the same time stimulated; sometimes he arrives unpleasantly overtired and over-stimulated. He is entitled to a good lunch or snack and a chance to relax. Homecoming is, in fact, a recuperative period in the cycle of activity and rest which his school day has set in motion. So if you have made plans for the rest of his day, if he is going to a friend's house to play or a friend is coming to his house, or if he is going out into a neighborhood of kids, give him a chance first to catch his breath and get his bearings.

Part Three

The Experiences in School

Far more important than the periods your child spends in work, in music, and in physical exercise each day is the *totality of experience* he undergoes and absorbs. Because he learns through his senses, his academic program in the first year of school is made up of a vast number of planned and casual experiences—experiences that the teacher plans for him and experiences that simply happen. They come about with no respect for the "schedule." Mathematics can no more be kept out of snack time than music can be kept out of art time.

Before specific experiences are enumerated, it is important to consider this totality of experience toward which your child is headed and which, in fact, he has already begun to accumulate. To understand *how* he is going to learn, let us look at *what* he is going to learn—in a broad, far-reaching philosophical sense.

1

Toward Learning Concepts

Most teachers and child-behavior specialists today tend to believe that behavior grows and changes in a patterned way, just as the body grows and changes. Another group believes that the pattern can be changed and that learning can be forced. There is controversy about how much you or a teacher can do to speed up or change your child's patterns of growth. However, as the parent of a school beginner, you don't have to worry about this. What you are doing now is probably good and sufficient. One hopes that you are providing the most rich and fruitful environment you can for your child—that you talk to him, read to him, play and listen to music with him, and so on. But it is not up to you at this moment to try to do anything special or different which will make him smarter or more mature. Your child will learn through his experiences at home and at school.

At school your child is going to learn concepts. The following is a short summary of some of the key concepts your child may glean from the learning experiences his teacher will help him through. She will not, of course, teach concepts explicitly. Probably she will never say, "Arithmetic is a language," but over the course of many weeks and months your child will come to know that arithmetic is a language, and he will learn to sort and sift all kinds of mathematical information into their proper conceptual relationships.

Discovery of key concepts is its own reward.

Before he gets locked into thinking of arithmetic in terms of the decimal system alone, before he learns by rote any number of other systems he will begin to learn the meaning of systems or **sets**, perhaps without thinking of them as math at all. For example, when he learns to tell the time, he will learn a number set based on 12; he will learn, in effect, that 10 plus 4 is not 14 but 2. When the class marks the calendar, he will learn a number set that is based on 7 if he is talking about a week, but one based on 30 or 31 (or 28 in February unless it is leap year) depending on what month it is. When he learns to use a rule and a yardstick, he will learn a number set based on 12 or on 3 or on 36; and as he learns to measure weight or count money he will learn other sets.

Moreover, he will learn that once he understands the set or the system, he can always work out an answer even if part of a statement in the language of arithmetic is missing. If he knows that he is dealing with hours on a clock, he knows what to expect when 6 plus ? equals 2. If he knows that he is dealing with a week, he expects a different answer when 6 plus ? equals 2. (On the clock, 6 plus 8 equals 2. In days of the week, the sixth day plus 3 equals the second day.) He will know this because he has been taught not by rote but by a method that emphasizes the *meaning* of the arithmetic operation.

Your child's most effective means of learning will be exercised by the act of discovery. Rather than simply telling him what he should know, his teacher will lead him toward using logic and reasoning in examining whatever facts or weighing whatever evidence is before him, so that he arrives at insights. As learning by discovery increases his intellectual ability, he will be able to conceive of abstractions and generalizations. He will be able to pursue a line of inquiry and problem solving. In this process, which discovers the meanings and concepts at the bottom of complex masses of information, he will make such meanings and concepts memorable and thus available for future use. In addition—and this is perhaps the most profitable by-product of the process—he will learn that discovery is its own reward. It is stimulating, and it is fun. Furthermore, directly in proportion to his sense of excitement about discovery will come his sense of self-confidence in his own abilities.

One thing to keep in mind about discovery as the means of learning is that no area is exclusive to boys or girls. Stereotyping as to sex occurs less and less. Cooking or Little League are for whoever wants to get involved, and this attitude toward slightly older youngsters has its foundation in kindergarten.

2

Experiences with Creative Materials

In the first year of school, creativity permeates the day. Almost everything that occurs is "creative" in some way, whether it involves art, drama, music, science, social studies, or nature. But certain important experiences derive directly from so-called creative materials.

The three stages of creativity.

Your child's use of creative materials—and thus his creative expression itself—is sure to progress through three stages. The first is the manipulative or experimental. With whatever materials he had in hand—blocks, crayons, paints, clay—this began in infancy, and may continue into first grade. He is getting acquainted with the material or media, discovering whether it can be pounded, flattened, torn, piled up, scribbled upon, or daubed and getting great satisfaction from simply manipulating it. His second stage is the symbolic. He may have entered this phase at about the age of four, and it may continue until he is eight or nine. Now he begins to attach meaning to his purely manipulative creations as they begin to symbolize a feeling or an idea for him. He may pile up his blocks and call his creation a tower or line them in a row and announce that he has created a wall. Even though you see only a few scribbles, a number of circles may be labeled a merry-go-round by him.

The art work of most kindergartners during the early months of school is in the experimental or symbolic stage. You will see it brought home day after day, and reams or chunks of it will probably be created at home, too. Gradually you will notice the symbolism advancing. Objects that are recognizable will begin to appear, and relationships between objects will be discovered. Sometime during the first year of school, your child will probably pass to the third stage, as his efforts move from the symbolic to the realistic. However, there is nothing wrong with him if he waits another year or two or even until he is as old as nine to reach the realistic stage. In this phase, he will be concerned with proportion, perspective, and true color. He will be genuinely concerned with his ability to represent reality in the medium in which he is working.

The values of your child's experience with all creative materials are many. Through these materials, he has countless opportunities to express his ideas visually and to express his feelings. He develops co-ordination of mind, hand, and eye. He learns to use a variety of materials safely and to care for them. He shares materials as well as ideas, learning to respect others and their efforts as well as himself and his own efforts. He begins to know when and how to obtain help and how to give and take honest criticism. And he concentrates on the problem at hand and thinks any problem through to solution.

Block building.

Blocks are one of the most creative materials. Block building develops motor co-ordination, establishes good work habits, and encourages social growth and co-operation. Concepts of size, quantity, and balance develop from working with large and small blocks, ranging from ten by fourteen inches or so down to two inches, with accompanying boards. Lifting, piling, and moving blocks not only exercise your child's arm, back, and leg muscles but also challenge him with problem-solving situations. Probably at the beginning of the school year he will prefer to build with blocks by himself. Taking them down will be as absorbing as putting them up, with his interest in a specific work project lasting through only one work period. As the year goes on, however, he will welcome others to his block building. Small groups will work together, and, as attention spans lengthen, the construction activities of the group will extend over several days. Having moved from the manipulative or experimental stage to the symbolic stage, they will create a house or store or school or airport, a swimming pool or airplane or space vehicle. At this stage, other creative materials often join whatever has been created from blocks. Toys and articles made from clay, plasticine, paper, or papier-mâché or realistic items turned out at the workbench may enhance and enrich the dramatic play that goes on in the block corner.

Woodworking.

Not every school goes in for woodworking in the kindergarten. Those that do realize that it is easier and more rewarding for children to work with sharp tools of good quality than with toy tools and that they enjoy learning how to use tools correctly. Experimenting with wood, creating simple objects, discovering texture and grain and qualities of hardness or softness, learning how a vise or a brace and bit work—these experiences add greatly to your child's perceptive powers. This activity is no more limited to boys, by the way, than playing house is limited to girls.

Modeling materials: From caveman to engineer.

Among three-dimensional creative materials, blocks and woodworking provide experiences in assembly, whether experimental, symbolic, or realistic. But a number of modeling materials give important experience in plasticity. Clay was probably the first manipulative material of the cave-dwelling four-year-old, and it has lost none of its charm in the eons since then. The very fact of its difference from plasticine provides your child with an interesting experience in chemistry, for the object he creates from clay will become permanent if he leaves it in the air to dry, while plasticine never dries. Play dough, if it is made from scratch from salt, flour, water, and perhaps a little alum powder as a preservative, gives an even broader experience of chemistry before little fingers begin to manipulate it. Papier-mâché is not something to tackle on the first day of school, as it calls for more supervision from the teacher than the other modeling materials and requires considerable time and skill from the pupil. Probably it will turn up late in the year when a study project is under way or when your child has a special individual project afoot.

Your child's experiences with modeling materials will be several. He begins with the manipulative, developing three-dimensional co-ordination of eye and hand. He creates objects both symbolic and realistic out of his manipulative experience of rolling, pounding, flattening, hollowing, poking, and smoothing. He learns a certain amount of engineering in joining two pieces together and of chemistry in painting, firing in a kiln, glazing, and refiring.

Sand.

A much less permanent three-dimensional material is sand. In classroom or on playground, the sandbox provides valuable experiences in measuring and weighing, digging and sifting, and wet sand is molded to make temporary objects. Equally important is sand's value as a medium for dramatic play; as much pretending goes on in the sandbox as in the block or doll corner.

Waste materials are put to use.

The three-dimensional world includes a host of waste materials—paper boxes, cones, cylinders, tubes, plates, bottle caps, yarns, raffia, string, buttons, fur, spools, pipe cleaners, post cards, coat hangers. Almost any design or picture that can be liberated from its background of paper or cloth by a pair of scissors can be used with paste or thread to enhance some object symbolically or realistically. In this way your child may produce a fancy wastebasket or a pencil container for his Daddy's desk, a personalized shoebox in which to store his treasures, a personalized Halloween mask or hand puppet, a set of coffee-can bongo drums, a cereal-box doll cradle, or a nearly three-dimensional collage to hang on the wall.

The right size crayon.

Probably, your child's first two-dimensional creative material was crayon and paper. Hardly anyone arrives at school without some prior experience with crayons. Unfortunately, most such experience is with the standard 3½- by 5/16-inch crayon that is sold everywhere. It is too small for the limited small-muscle control achieved by most preschoolers. Much better is the large 4½- by ½-inch crayon that is supplied in most kindergartens. Equally unfortunate is too much use of crayons or their use in tracing around patterns or coloring inside the outlines of coloring books or sheets dittoed by a teacher. Such pattern filling will discourage your child's creativity and stifle his initiative. Prehistoric man had no coloring books; yet he found his way through the manipulative, symbolic, and realistic phases in the use of whatever creative materials he could devise.

Paints and painting.

When it comes to painting, your child's teacher may start him off without paint. The experience of painting on a chalkboard with clear water will give him an excellent introduction to the use of the paintbrush as he learns to control dripping by stroking the brush against the side of the container and discovers the variety of effects he can achieve by using the tip, the edge, or the flat side of the brush. Water painting seems almost silly to grownups, but to one with little experience of the brush it is fascinating. It avoids for the moment the complex issue of what color to use, and half the fun comes from the magical disappearance of the creation as it evaporates—a science experience your child's teacher will find worth noting and expanding upon. This alone explains how impossible it is to separate art from science.

Aside from the creations he produces, the various kinds of paint give your child experiences in mixing and chemistry. Tempera or poster paint comes in the bottle ready to use, or is mixed from powder and water to the consistency of light cream. Inexpensive and colorful, it encourages large, free work with a long-handled brush. Plastic paint is similar in opacity and use, but because the brush can be wiped clean on a wet sponge, your child learns that he can go from one color to another without changing brushes or washing them. If he uses enamel or flat house paint at the workbench, on the other hand, he discovers the world of varnish brushes, of turpentine and thinner, more difficult to clean up. When the finger paints come out, he is introduced (if he is invited to make up the medium from scratch) to the creative and chemical possibilities of liquid starch or wallpaper paste and the colored powder paint he mixed before, plus glazed shelf or butcher paper he has seen at home or in the meat market. With finger painting, he discovers the infinite capacity for design that nature has bestowed on him.

Finger painting is often a rhythmic activity. Big, sweeping movements help release emotional tension with great satisfaction. Finger painting to music often leads to more general, creative body movements to music. Your child may discover his willingness to express a feeling for music more easily this way than in direct response. His hands and fingers, having experienced an enjoyable freedom of expression while creating with finger paints, may respond eagerly to finger plays and finger dramatization proposed by his teacher. These can range from the good old "Here is the church and here is the steeple" or "Where is pointer?" to hand puppets and finger puppets.

The infinite variety of dramatic play.

Dramatization, of course, is never ending and never the same. Dramatic play springs spontaneously from building with blocks, from the sandbox, and from the modeling materials. It is developed into more meaningful experiences as records and songs are dramatized with a suggestion of costume—a hat or scarf, a cane or spectacles—and as field trips to store or firehouse are recreated or the flannel board becomes the focus for cutouts especially prepared by the pupils. Dramatization through the creative materials that he himself has mixed, painted, cut out, stacked, and modeled is far more rewarding than through ready-made commercial products. Your young puppeteer will probably express himself better through a face he has drawn on cardboard, cut out, and attached to a tongue depressor than through a fancy puppet from the toy store.

Dramatic play raises the question of the audience—often the adult who criticizes instead of accepting and encouraging. One of the main points of working with creative materials is for your child to be free to investigate, to manipulate, and to create. This means that he must have a wide variety of materials and plenty of ideas to express. The ideas come from all the experiences he undergoes—not just special excursions, stories, songs. At the same time, the *process* of creation probably will give your child as much satisfaction as the finished product, if not more. Often he will be able to wash his hands of some marvelous creation, both literally and figuratively, as soon as it is completed and will have no interest whatever in saving it. We may say that he is drawing realistically without necessarily meaning that he draws what he actually sees. He may paint a realistic dog in an unrealistic bright orange color because he wants to draw a happy dog, and bright orange is, for him, a happy color. Or he may draw the round top of a man's head and then draw a hat over it, so that the head is seen through the hat. This makes eminent sense to him, for he knows perfectly well that the head is in the hat and has so drawn it. His teacher will accept these expressions of feeling and of experience at their face value, knowing how easy it would be to crimp his style and his creativity by imposing adult values on his work. Though he may have walked away from it with nonchalance, she will occasionally put his work on display, knowing the pride and pleasure and additional experience he will gain from seeing his work as part of the décor of the room.

Putting art on display.

Displays include art-appreciation materials. These range from famous paintings to colorful autumn leaves, from a small flower garden in a corner to a short series of art slides and films, from glass paperweights to replicas of famous sculpture. Displayed at the eye level of the children, such objects lead to discussion and experience in areas other than art. A famous painting may reflect a specific bygone era as well as demonstrate the timelessness of a masterpiece and so help provide an experience and understanding of historical time. Art-appreciation materials, in addition to the creations of the pupils in the room, make more valuable displays than highly colored commercial pictures of farm animals and nursery-rhyme characters.

3

Experiences Involving Language and Literature

Your child is going off to school able to speak and comprehend his language fairly well. A year from now he will be ready to write it and to read it, and in fact will probably already have learned something of reading and writing. Speaking, hearing, reading, and writing are learned skills. This means that they can be improved, and the chief purpose of learning them and improving them is not merely for your child to arrive at the ability to learn to read but for him to gain the desire to read to learn. To develop that desire is the ultimate goal of the multitude of experiences he will have in language and literature in kindergarten.

Creating the need and desire to communicate.

If he is to grasp and express ideas, the kindergartner needs some abilities and skills that come before reading itself. Even before he masters these skills, he needs acceptance as he is. To help him develop his sense of security, his teacher will keep in mind that his beginning attempts to express ideas to the group are more important than the way they are expressed. He may be in the habit of using a comfortable "home dialect" that works fine among his intimates. As time goes by, she will help him grow in his ability to use and hear a more standard language. This expansion of his skill will include a number of growth factors. His vocabulary will increase to suit his increasing needs and interests. His facility in oral expression will grow. He will learn the mechanics of reading a book from left to right, top to bottom, front to back. His ability to sustain his listening power will extend to fifteen to twenty minutes. He will develop the visual discrimination to see similarities and differences in size, shape, and color, and the auditory acuity to hear similarities and differences in speech sounds and in the sounds around him.

The values derived from your child's experiences in the language arts will be many. Over the year, as his imagination is stimulated and his individuality of expression encouraged, his activities will create within him the need and desire to communicate with other children and adults. He will develop a rich fund of meaningful concepts that stimulate conversation. His interest in new words will be stimulated, too, and with his increased vocabulary will come an improved ability to enunciate and pronounce words correctly, to use correct speech habits and complete sentences, and to speak clearly and audibly with a pleasing voice. You will find that he can tell well-known stories in sequence and that he has begun to learn the habit of orderly thinking and the ability to keep to the point. He will even have developed the habit of listening with attention.

Language develops self-worth.

Perhaps the most significant value of these experiences will come in the area of personal development. Language shapes values, and the ability to handle it helps your child develop feelings of self-worth and respect and promotes his understanding of others. Because speech itself is a form of behavior that expresses personality and helps to develop it, he grows daily and develops a favorable self-concept as he is able daily to tell of his own experiences.

The values to be derived from one group experience in the language arts are exemplified in what happened in one California school when the kindergarten was given a set of pans in a large box with a transparent Pliofilm "window" in the box top. One child picked up the top, held it in front of her and made funny faces through it. Several children laughed and told the teacher, "Debra made a TV." The teacher saw at once the germ of a learning experience and encouraged the class to figure out how to make the box lid look more like a TV set. The children decided to thumbtack it to the top of a wooden box so that all could be seen behind it in turn. An extra-dividend creative experience came with nailing two large wooden beads loosely to the wooden box for changing channels and volume, while the frame of the box cover was covered with paper to hide some small pictures printed on it. In addition, a number exercise put figures 1 through 10 on a circle behind one of the beads. The "TV set" was used to announce daily news, for solo and even quartet singing, and for story telling. Stocking puppets and paper hand puppets made in class appeared on it. It helped timid children to speak and sing. Even the teacher was surprised that when someone could not be heard and the other children asked if they might turn up the volume, the performer then spoke or sang more loudly. Speaking in complete sentences, enunciation, and pronunciation improved when the pupils were "on TV." They learned graphically the importance of looking at the audience while speaking or singing and of listening attentively to the performer. The fun lasted without boredom from February to May.

Experiences with language and literature range from oral expression to the improvement of speech, from listening to "reading" from the classics. In order to get a clear look at them, they will be examined here one by one, but in the same way as creative materials, they overlap and merge and happen continuously in the classroom.

Oral expression is everywhere.

The time for oral expression begins when the first child enters the classroom and ends when the last one goes home. Oral accompaniment enters all kindergarten activities. The wide variety of experiences your child has in speaking in a single day are of two main types: informal situations which call for speaking face to face with one or two individuals and organized situations which involve speaking to a larger group or audience. Vocabulary development is part and parcel of all experiences in oral expression. Language games include conversations using toy telephones and telling personal experiences through hand or stick puppets, along with imitative performances by the children. The teacher often selects a child to describe a person or object in the room so that the others can guess who or what is described. At dismissal time she may announce in turn, "All boys wearing brown shoes may go, all girls wearing red shoes may go," and so on until only two or three are left. She may then break them up completely with "All children with two ears may go" or some other designation that is, to them, hilarious.

Games and nursery rhymes.

More complicated language games develop as the year goes on. Synonym-antonym games involve the teacher's saying a word and your child's saying a word that means the same or opposite. Preposition games mean putting an object in, on, under, beside, below, above, or behind a box. Adverb games direct the players to walk quickly, slowly, sadly, quietly, or noisily, while adjective games tell them to find objects big, little, hard, smooth, blue, red, or striped or to pretend that they are big, little, happy, brave, kind, old, or young.

There are rhymes and finger plays to help oral expression. These often come together, to reinforce each other, as in

Open, close them.
Open, close them.
Give a little clap.
Open, close them.
Open, close them.
Fold them in your lap.

Or in

Thumb is one, have some fun.
Pointer two, I see you.
Tall man three, like a tree.
Ring man four, now one more.
Thumpy five, swim and dive.

The good old nursery rhymes—"Little Miss Muffet," "Little Jack Horner," "Humpty Dumpty," or "Hey Diddle Diddle"—serve equally well to stimulate your child's enjoyment of the likenesses and differences in sound and encourage him to discover for himself words that rhyme. Often the teacher will tell a favorite rhyme and stop when she comes to the second of the rhyming words in order to let the children put in the right one. In order to emphasize sounds which many children find difficult, she may often lead them in repeating special rhymes such as this one, which exercises the difficult consonants and blends, including *f, z, l, th, wh, v,* and *r:*

Fuzzy little caterpillar,
Crawling, crawling on the ground!
Fuzzy little caterpillar,
Nowhere, nowhere to be found,
Though we've looked and looked and hunted
Everywhere around!

Stories and riddles.
Another way in which difficult sounds are practiced is in stories and riddles. The teacher may call for add-on stories, in which several children in turn create new twists in a plot launched by the teacher, and open-end stories, in which one pupil completes a story, usually a familiar one, told by the teacher or by a classmate. Riddles give experience in recognizing significant characteristics of objects and help your youngster to gain power in quick, accurate thinking. They also give him a boost when he guesses the correct answer. Riddles may be very simple: "Moo, moo, moo, moo. I like to eat grass. I am a ———." Or more complicated: "I am white. I wear feathers. I have an orange bill and feet. Mickey Mouse is my friend. Who am I?" Or slightly ambiguous: "I have four legs and can swim. I move slowly. I hide in the mud all winter. I eat insects and flies. Who am I?" Or less bucolic and more urban: "I have a front door and a back door. But I am not a

house, for I can move through the busy city streets carrying many people at the same time.''

One of the most important experiences your child will have in oral expression will come when he feels enough rapport with his teacher to relate some complete experience to her. It may be part fiction or fantasy. It may be quite scientific, explaining some discovery or deduction he has found out for himself. The teacher will discern the elements of an interesting, coherent story, and may offer to write it down and print it later on chart paper, asking your child if he wants to illustrate it.

The important thing is that it is *his* story. The ideas are his, and the symbols that his teacher uses to preserve it are matched to his ideas. He is being introduced to symbols—the mechanical tools of written expression, including spelling, printing, punctuation, capitalization, and paragraphing—that express his own thinking. He sees his oral expression turn into written expression, and he knows, even if he is not yet able to read it, that this story expresses his ideas.

Speaking in chorus.

Then there is choral speaking. The shy child is drawn out, the garrulous contained, when they speak in unison. Vocabulary is built, a sense of rhythm and inflection developed, diction improved, and memory stimulated by this group endeavor and responsibility. The teacher starts things off by asking the group to join in the refrain. ''Jack, be nimble, Jack, be quick!'' she says, and the crowd responds, ''Jack, jump over the candlestick!'' When refrain responses have become second nature, she divides the group into sections for two-part choral speaking. Especially good are selections that ask a question and get an answer: Group One says, ''Pussy cat, pussy cat, where have you been?'' and Group Two replies, ''I've been to London to visit the queen.'' Finally, the soloists emerge as each child takes one line and the group joins in the refrain.

Dramatic play has been mentioned previously, as it occurs spontaneously in work with creative materials. This exercise in oral expression calls for a brief planning session to decide on the casting of roles and the use of suggested costumes or settings, but informality is the key to success. What counts is the vehicle. Familiar rhymes and stories from ''Mother Goose'' and her associates, including ''The Three Bears,'' ''The Three Little Pigs,'' ''The Three Billy Goats Gruff'' or, to get away from triads and into a triangle, ''Little Red Riding Hood,'' work very well in giving your child the experience of cutting loose before the crowd to demonstrate, for instance, how the father bear sounded when he saw that somebody had been sampling his porridge.

If you're concerned about speech correction . . .

You may be concerned about speech correction. If your child is not pronouncing all the speech sounds correctly by the time he goes to school, it may be for any of several reasons. His teacher will note the problem and, knowing the importance of correct speech to his social and emotional adjustment, will work to help him without making him self-conscious about it. Most kids this age enjoy playing with words and sounds, and she will exploit this natural tendency to improve his ability to distinguish sounds and to enunciate accurately.

There are two types of speech handicap: physical and functional. Physical handicaps include organic conditions, such as defective hearing, cleft palate, tied tongue, enlarged tonsils, adenoids, malocclusion, stuttering, and stammering. Functional handicaps are infantile speech, careless speech habits, and lack of voice control. Since either kind may have a psychological effect on personality as well as on academic progress—if your child is sensitive about defective speech he may hold back on expressing himself orally—the teacher will get in touch with the school nurse and the speech therapist in all cases of physical handicap and in any where psychological problems seem to be looming.

Baby talk.

Infantile speech is baby talk. It is the substitution, omission, or addition of certain speech sounds. *T* is substituted for *c*, *th* for *s* or for *f*, *w* for *v*, and so on. *R* is left out after consonant sounds, or *l* and *y* in initial position in words are omitted. The teacher's constant repetition, in the correct form, of what the child has said incorrectly (casually and without self-consciousness on either part) is the best method of correcting baby talk. Many children in kindergarten show infantile speech to some degree. The teacher knows that most are already beginning to outgrow it and need no therapy and that the less self-consciousness the better. If, on the other hand, the child has begun to be self-critical, she will want to do something about it.

Learning to listen.

Your child listened before he spoke; listening was his first communications skill. However, his natural growth in the art of speaking and his natural egocentricism may by now have produced an urge to be heard rather than to hear. He may listen without paying attention and, really, without hearing. Therefore, along with oral expression, he will undergo experiences in effective listening.

His teacher is aware that everything from hunger and fatigue to room ventilation and temperature may influence his listening. She knows that in order to learn he must be able to listen appreciatively to stimuli that please his senses and with discrimination to informative speech; he must be able also to listen to the ideas of others in a group and to listen critically in order to evaluate what is being said. Listening to directions and following them will be developed as the children and teacher take turns conducting games such as "Simon Says." Immediate recall is fostered by "Going to Boston," in which the first child says, "I am going to Boston and I will take a hat," the second says, "I am going to Boston and I will take a hat and a scarf," and so on. Delayed recall may mean answering questions about a story that was read yesterday or summarizing what was told by a classroom visitor or seen and heard in a filmstrip or sound film. Countless other games involve children in hiding by being located by sound, in echoing phrases spoken by the teacher, in identifying familiar indoor and outdoor sounds, in imitating machines or animals, and in lining up and being dismissed on certain word or sound cues.

Literature: from Homer to Curious George.

Literature is not confined to Tolstoy and Macbeth; it is also Dr. Seuss and Curious George. Literature in the kindergarten involves story telling, poetry, and picture books, as well as learning to use the library.

Our very earliest literature combined, in the works of Homer, story telling with poetry, and no generation since his time has failed to enjoy listening to and telling stories. While the teacher's general aim in telling stories is to give her kindergartners enjoyment in good literature by arousing their joy, surprise, and wonder, she also has more specific aims. One of the first learning experiences your child will get from story time is that of sharing pleasure with a group. The vicarious experience is important, since it brings an understanding of other parts of the world, of other people, of other times, and of the similarities among all peoples.

The stories themselves cover a wide range, from the traditional folk tales such as "The Little Red Hen" or "The Three Bears" to realistic stories about contemporary life involving ships or airplanes and the men who run them, from animal stories and nature stories to the traditional stories that dramatize Christmas, Thanksgiving, or patriotic holidays.

Mother Goose is back.

Poetry appeals to your child's natural love of rhyme. He will get a kick out of nonsense rhymes, and he will make up short, original rhymes. Knowing that he enjoys rhythm as well as rhyme, his teacher will probably read him plenty of free verse. As his work with creative materials goes into the realistic phase, he will probably enjoy illustrating his favorite poems.

It is interesting to note that Mother Goose, who was "out" for a while, is back "in." She has been revived with enthusiasm in the kindergarten curriculum, probably because nowhere else in literature is there such a collection of rhymes and riddles, counting rhymes and tongue twisters, lullabies and nonsense so pertinent to the age and to the language-arts experiences that are needed. Contemporary poems which reflect, with a childlike quality, everyday life and an appreciation of animals or the sun and stars or carrots and onions usually have literary value, and these are used in the classroom. The teacher's chief headache, in choosing poetry for class, is to distinguish between poems written for children and poems written about children. Many that pretend to be for are really about, for the amusement of grownups.

Books develop visual discrimination.

For a five-year-old, pictures often are the story; so when the teacher reads to the class, she will make sure that all can see the pictures. It is when a small group is semicircled around her that she begins to awaken an interest in attractive books. She will use those with bright, colorful illustrations that show plenty of action and a minimum of detail. She will begin early in the year to instill the idea that books, including picture stories, provide information as well as entertainment.

Your child's appreciation of the functional use of books will be developed further as he is encouraged to make his own original picture books to illustrate class projects or interests of his own, and the experience will involve a related experience with creative materials.

To match letters takes a certain visual discrimination, which will be exercised and developed by numerous experiences. The difference between individual letters and individual words is often very small. If your child is to discriminate between them, he needs a great deal of experience in seeing differences in objects, colors, sizes, and shapes. Games in which he must observe likenesses and differences in objects, in spectrum colors, in circles on the wall, and in types of objects assembled together (round objects together, square objects together, beads and shells sorted by type, size, and color) are vital preparation for learning the alphabet.

At last he will be let in on the secret that the letters he sees have names. The teacher may hold up a cutout of a letter, and say, "This letter is at the beginning of someone's first name. If it is the letter that begins your first name, you may stand up." Name cards will come next, and letters will be lined up in a pocket chart or along the chalk rail to spell names. However, the ability to discriminate between letters will have come from countless comparisons of sizes and shapes.

Related experiences will develop auditory discrimination. Listening, hand clapping, marching, jingling, drum beating, record playing, and so on are experiences to help young ears learn to distinguish subtleties of similar sound. Thus your child will begin to get ready to match words that start alike in both letter and sound, and to distinguish between those that sound as if they start alike but don't ("cinch" and "sing"), and those that look as if they start alike but don't ("cinch" and "catch").

Becoming aware of the need for writing.

Through all his experiences in the language arts, your child will gradually become aware of the need for writing. He will find himself asking to have oral expressions recorded and written expressions interpreted. He will carry written communications between home and school, classroom and office, his classroom and other classrooms, and will discover the pleasure of receiving written messages and letters from others. Everywhere he turns he will see the need for and use of writing. He will begin to burn with the urge to put letters to work making words, and words to work carrying ideas.

He will begin also to have the experience of composition, of authoring, of creating a whole that is more than a word or sentence. His awareness will embrace the background sources of group expressions of thought—the sights and sounds, scents and tastes, stories and discussion and study trips that may be organized into a written work. Planning the topic and the ground to be covered, dictating the thoughts and seeing the teacher record them on paper or on the chalk board, evaluating what she has put down and pulling together sentences that belong together while cutting out repetition, then checking to see that the idea has been expressed and rewording the sentences as needed—these are separate experiences as well as parts of one great experience that will help to give your child skill in the language arts.

4

Experiences Involving Social Studies

Social studies in the first year of school have two aspects. First, the learning experiences give your child some of the skills and attitudes he needs in working and playing with others his age. Second, they give him basic concepts about how people in their homes and communities and around the world live and work.

Rights, sharing and turns.
Just about everything that happens during the kindergarten day is some kind of social experience. In social activities that are a part of social studies, your child learns to respect the rights of classmates, share materials, take turns, listen to the ideas of others and express ideas to others, obey the rules of the school, and respect the adults in charge. Additional social experiences are such events as the snack period, a birthday or Halloween party, a visit to another class, or an invitation to others to visit the kindergarten. They relate ultimately to the concept of self that arises from your child's awareness of the attitudes others hold toward him and the responses they make to him. His concept of self helps to govern his ability to live with others.

Study of his own environment—family, school, and neighborhood or community—foreshadows study of the broader environments treated in the

64

disciplines of history, geography, economics, sociology, political science, and anthropology. While most of these will be studied as disciplines in later grades of school and in college, they are included as concepts in simplified form in many a kindergarten today.

Your child learns facts in order to organize them into concepts. An appreciation of how Mr. Piersall's market works or of how Mr. Gearhart's newspaper gets printed is not the end but the means. The values derived are in seeing relationships, in clarifying misconceptions, in orienting information about time and distance, in reaching a basic understanding about the world around him.

The second half of the definition of social studies (the basic concept of how people live and work) is applicable to some of the learning experiences that will probably occur in your child's first year of school. The early experiences in social studies will be mainly in the classroom and centered on the concept of the family, but later field trips and visits from interesting people will enlarge the scope of interest to the neighborhood and to the community at large.

The family as a social concept.

You might as well face it: There is no telling what your child is likely to say about his family while he is in school. However, good teachers are somewhat like priests and doctors in tending to forget which individual has confessed which sin. Your child's teacher will encourage him to talk about his family, to name brothers and sisters and count the members of his family, to draw pictures of his home or build it with blocks or model it in clay. She will do this because the family may not yet be obvious in its concept or meaning, even though it is the biggest single totality in his experience. She works to make him conscious of his own family in size and composition and similarity to or difference from other families, and to make the class aware of different kinds of families and cultures represented within the room. The experiences of conversation and discussion, of recreating the family either symbolically or realistically on paper or in blocks or clay or (perhaps most important of all) in dramatic play in the doll corner or sandbox or in a story dictated to the teacher, are the means by which the concept of family is established.

Then the group.

As he begins to understand the meaning of the family and the differences among families, your child will also begin to get the idea of the group and the differences among groups. What he is part of in September is a mass of children; by October or November the mass will have settled down into groups which are ever reorganizing: the block crowd, the sandbox gang, the doll-corner children, the story-time group, the science-project group. Never quite the same two days in a row, each group is always an identifiable group. The teacher will encourage the class to be aware, through discussion, dramatization, the source material, of other outside groups to which her pupils belong, in church or neighborhood or social club. A Friday dismissal-time discussion or a Monday arrival-time conversation, for instance, might identify any number of such groups, as various children talk of a Sunday-school picnic or church fair, a neighborhood block party, a family holiday party, or a chartered bus trip.

The neighborhood is a laboratory.

Beyond the school lies its neighborhood, a first-rate social-studies laboratory. Usually a complex neighborhood surrounds the city school. In the suburbs or a small town, the immediate neighborhood may be made up entirely of residential buildings, and the neighborhood must be considered to be the more widespread community. Field trips will take your child to see firehouse, supermarket, and post office, while back in the classroom he will reconstruct the school neighborhood or a shopping center in blocks or create a farm with foam-rubber trees, papier-mâché cabbages, and clay figures.

What he will be building up to is geography. The association of physical and cultural features of an area, the concept of the region and the map—these are achieved by learning experiences involving the neighborhood and the community. From them to the concept of the globe is a big leap, but it is a leap that is made gradual and easy—by floor plans of the classroom; by the school building made three-dimensional with blocks; by neighborhood maps, which introduce the idea that a map is a kind of picture that shows how familiar places and areas are related; and by maps of the city, county, state, and country. Finally, these various maps will be compared with the globe, and your child's country, state, and city or regional area will be located on it.

How long ago? How far away?

The globe is the natural introduction to the concept of space and time. Kindergartners already know much of planets, astronauts, and orbits. They are familiar with the earth's rotation and its movement around the sun; with such paraphernalia as globe, tennis-ball moon, flashlight sun, and darkened room, they delight in reconstructing our segment of the universe and in seeing how time and climate and seasonal changes are dictated by the positions of planet and star. (Such work is, of course, simultaneously a science experience.)

They learn the passage of time, for instance, from egg timers that tell them when a turn has expired, and they learn the process of change by repeated trips to the site of a building under construction or a neighborhood under redevelopment. Or the teacher may bring an older person from the community into the classroom to talk about changes since his or her youth.

Family snapshots of parents or grandparents in outdated clothing and settings may help introduce the idea of historical time.

"Long ago" is, to a five-year-old, the year before he was born and the time when the Pilgrims landed. It is hard for him to conceive of the vast extent of chronological time. One help is the time line—a line taped or marked on the floor, or a rope tied with knots, each mark or knot denoting a year of his life. When he has grasped the idea of the time line, a much longer line is introduced (perhaps extending across the classroom), and he learns that its marks or knots stand for important historical events, such as Columbus's discovery of America or the landing of the Pilgrims. Another help is the idea of historical periods; the class marks along the time line the period of the exploration of the New World or the period of the colonization of America. Such concepts are emphasized by visits to museums, explorations in books, audiovisual aids, and dramatic play.

What's happening today?

Current history, or current events, is another part of social studies in which learning experiences help to establish a broad concept. Your kindergartner's generation has seen all kinds of world events happening from the living room. He has been to countless news events. Now, in his classroom, the news will be used as an aid in developing speaking and writing skills and as another kind of social-studies experience. Chances are that he will be asked to report news sometime. An example of this is the class that rigged a "TV set" from a see-through box lid. Your child's class may maintain a newspaper or cut news pictures from a daily paper. The globe and maps will be used to orient the news geographically, whether it tells of a fire downtown or an earthquake in Asia.

Producing and buying and selling.

Your five-year-old has seen thousands of advertising messages and made hundreds of trips to stores of all kinds. He has probably handled some money and made some purchases of his own, and it is likely that he has heard the phrases "too expensive" or "we can't afford." He has watched buyer and seller at work. All have been experiences in economics, but they have probably not given him a basic meaning or concept of economics. His kindergarten experiences in social studies can give him such a concept, and it is one that will stand him in good stead as long as he lives.

Take what happened in one New York City kindergarten. An extended study project examined New York's food supply. It began with the teacher's reading a book about supermarkets and the class's composing a letter that asked parents to take the children along on the next family marketing trip. The children reported many experiences and much detailed factual information from their observations. After a week or so, a play-store counter was brought into the classroom, and when some tentative and spontaneous play with props from the doll corner had aroused interest in playing store, props such as empty food cartons and cans, pictures of food, shopping bags, cash-register tapes, play money, advertising posters, price signs and labels, coin changers, pocketbooks, telephones, pencils, and pads were added. Extremely simple 8-mm. movies showed supermarket workers at their jobs and trucks delivering and unloading food at the store—and added the interesting manipulative experience of operating the self-threading projector. A couple of more ambitious educational films told about where our food comes from and how machines and tools help us. By now the children could describe a variety of supermarket jobs, such as bringing food into the store, cutting meat, putting prices on food, or working the cash register, but most of them played only two roles: storekeeper or customer. Although, initially, many of them thought that it was the storekeeper or checker who paid the customer, by the time (a few weeks later) when the class walked to a nearby supermarket to buy the ingredients to make cookies, they had not only straightened out the roles of buyer and seller but had grasped the concept of consumers as people who need and use goods and services and producers as people who work to earn money, usually producing goods and services. A culminating experience was the visit of the supermarket manager to the class, when he gave further details about jobs.

This led to ideas about money and prices. The children grasped such concepts as the function of the cash register and its tape, the exchange of money for goods, the need for making change, and some notion of money denominations and relative values. At first, however, the use of money in the play store was purely manipulative. No matter what amount of play money the customer tendered, he got change. This was not surprising, for very few number concepts had yet been established—and, besides, manipulating change is fun.

It was hoped that a cooky sale, with real money and realistic prices, would pin down the concepts of profit and change making. The children decided to determine cooky prices by vote, and the result was a net loss. Confronted with the money receipts from the cooky sale, they did not remember that they had spent money on ingredients, nor how much they had spent. They simply assumed that the money taken in was all profit. The experience in this case involved a concept that had *not* been learned.

A second sale involved hard-boiled eggs to decorate at Easter. The children borrowed one dollar from a frequent visitor, sold eggs for six cents, carefully counted out the four-penny change from dimes, paid back their lender, and made a profit which they voted to spend on jellybeans. This time they understood that there was money left over. However, though they were getting the idea of costs, their delineation of the concept of profit was still not entirely clear beyond the idea that it was money left over.

And then—the division of labor.

Egg-coloring activity led to the making of paper flower baskets and to an interesting experience in the division of labor. The class as a whole was shown how to make a basket, and a race was then held between two groups. In one, children worked individually, each child cutting and pasting each part and assembling his basket. In the other group, some cut handles, some cut slits, some cut flowers, some pasted, and some assembled. When time was called, the six children in the first group had made six baskets, while the six children in the second group had made twelve baskets. The experience was remembered long afterward as an example of how the division of labor in manufacturing increases productivity—though not, of course, in such pompous language.

5

Experiences Involving Science and Nature

Why does boiling water bubble? What makes the egg inside the shell get hard? Your five-year-old wants to know how and why. His teacher, though she will not spring Boyle's law on him, will be ready several times a day to help him get the factual answers to his questions and, at the same time, to help him understand the basic processes of science. She will lead him through learning experiences which tell him that scientific knowledge is developed and verified by looking at physical phenomena and at the relationships among them and that science is a way of describing or explaining such phenomena.

A mode of inquiry—not a body of knowledge.

The chief value your child will gain from his learning experiences in science will be his understanding that science is not a body of knowledge but a mode of inquiry. It is the method of observing a phenomenon or recognizing a problem, formulating some possible solutions or working hypotheses, trying out or testing the suggested solutions, and arriving at one or more conclusions that can apply as well to other, similar situations. If your child's kindergarten science experiences teach him not only why snow melts indoors but how to meet new situations in daily living—such as how to figure out why snow melts indoors—they will have succeeded in their purpose.

Science experiences in kindergarten involve everything from stones to stars, from hamsters to hippos. Observation of living things is probably kindergarten's oldest science activity, but today it is combined with such varied areas of learning as weather and astronomy, magnetism and electricity, energy and physical and chemical change, rocks and minerals, and conservation. In all these cases the underlying concept of why and how something happens is more important than simply the observation of what happens.

Animal life.

Animal life is studied in the zoo, on the farm, and in the classroom. By observing hamsters, kittens, guppies, turtles, snakes, baby chicks, and parakeets kept temporarily in the classroom, your child discovers the needs and purposes served by fur, scales, and feathers. Methods of flying, running, crawling, or swimming are compared, feeding habits are watched, methods of sleep noted, egg laying and live birth compared. Usually animals cannot be kept long enough for complete life cycles to occur, except in such cases as the caterpillar, but major changes can be seen. As tadpoles become frogs and chicks chickens, the idea of change and cycle is established. Field trips to the zoo are combined with books, films, and other visual aids to extend the discovery of the world of fur, scales, and feathers and to broaden the concept of animals in nature and in the life of man.

Your five-year-old may make friends with a gerbil. His experience with this lively little animal will include the discovery that the gerbil consumes only a few drops of water in a week or more. He may also watch a cactus plant in a sunny corner of the classroom and learn, by testing his hypothesis that maybe too much water is bad for some plants, that a cactus can be killed by overwatering. When he discovers that the gerbil and the cactus are both following the dictates of the environment for which they were born—the desert—but that wherever they are, the gerbil somehow knows enough not to drink more water than his system needs while the cactus tries to absorb whatever water it is given, he will gain some powerful insights into nature.

Plant life.

If anyone has ever organized a Society for the Prevention of Cruelty to Plants, it has gone unnoticed. We do not seem to mind experimenting with plant life. What happens to a cactus if it is overwatered, to a geranium if it is left out in the cold, your child will be able to see for himself. He will be able to test the right and wrong conditions for reproduction and for the continuance of life. He will discover the need of plants for sun, water, air, soil, and food, all in varying amounts and degrees as they grow from seeds, bulbs, roots, stems, and leaves. He will probably watch a sweet potato grow in a glass jar, half a carrot in a bowl of water put out roots from the root that is itself, a flower spring up from seeds in soil. In a tasting party, he will himself eat roots (carrots), stalks (celery), leaves (lettuce), fruit (apple), and seed (pecan).

Weather.

As he notes its influence on plant life and animal life, he will discover weather. He will watch the thermometer and record its ups and downs, put water outdoors and see what happens to it when the temperature reaches freezing, keep a record of wind direction from the school weathervane, and a diary or calendar of sunny, gray, windy, rainy, and snowy days. If he takes a toy balloon home from a birthday party on a cold day and discovers that it shrinks outdoors and then expands again in the warm house, and then reports this phenomenon to his teacher, he may succeed in demonstrating the expansion and contraction of gases and solids in heat and cold—all as a result of observing the effects of weather.

The stars.

Your five-year-old's learning experiences in astronomy will be closely related to other learning experiences. The effect of heat and light upon plant life, the relative positions of earth and sun which cause changes in the seasons, the rotation of the earth and its movement in orbit by which we measure time (all of which we have discussed in previous pages) help to establish his concept of the celestial world. These observations may be bolstered by a field trip to a planetarium, a long look at the night sky through binoculars, and books and filmstrips illustrating our solar system and the universe.

Your child's comb, if he runs it through his hair several times, will afterward attract bits of paper. His birthday-party balloon, after being rubbed against his woolen sweater, will stick to the wall. Such commonplace magic opens the door to the idea that electricity is everywhere and that it reacts when conditions are right. The common reaction of the paper or balloon reveals the presence of electricity that just sits there (static electricity) on the surface of an object. From this concept it is an easy step to the concept of current electricity that flows in a wire.

Matter and energy.

Don't be surprised if you walk into your child's classroom one day just in time to see him standing on a chair and, with the teacher's approval, dropping a ball, a bucket of sand, a plate, a saucepan, and a handful of doll-corner silverware onto the floor. He will be observing and discovering whether each item bounces, breaks, flattens, spreads out, or piles up, and learning that matter is everything around him, in solid, liquid, or gas, and that as matter changes position or moves, it causes energy. If he has been exposed to magnets, he may soon talk of his magnet "working" to pull his tiny cork sailboat by its steel needle mast. He may come home and lecture you about the electrical wires that run from the pole in the street to the corner of your house, the endless energy that comes through those wires from far away and is ready to be put to work at each wall outlet, and the electrical energy that is changed to heat energy in your stove and to light energy in your lamps.

The idea of physical and chemical change will come easily to your child as he observes the evaporation of water—rapidly as his water painting on the chalk board disappears, or slowly as a puddle on the schoolyard pavement disappears. When a stoppered test tube half full of water is heated until it blows its top, the work that can be performed by a physical change is demonstrated. Some forms of matter, he will discover by applying the scientific method, do not change so easily. Heating rocks may crack them into fragments, but they will not melt or turn to steam. They have potential energy, he may learn, only when they are round and lie at the top of a hill.

The idea of change is one of the key concepts of science. It has two aspects which your child will understand through his learning experiences: Some change is reversible, and some is irreversible. He will discover that water may be changed to ice or to steam and back again in either direction, and that the kinetic energy which has been expended as a toy ran down may be stored up in it again by rewinding the toy. On the other hand, when a log has been burned in a fireplace, he may inform you that it has been changed irreversibly into heat and light.

In developing his concept of matter and of physical and chemical change, your child will also develop the concept of *material*. Where he may earlier have sorted by sets, distinguishing buttons from washers and nuts from pennies, he may now sort by material, distinguishing bone from mother-of-pearl or wood, and brass from steel. He will then be led to discover that some objects, such as nuts and bolts, chinaware or string, are made from only one material, while others, such as pencils and shoes, are made from several. In so describing and classifying objects by the attributes that he can observe about them, he will be practicing discovery and exercising his scientific thinking.

6

Experiences Involving
Number Concepts

You may already have discovered that your child knows how to count—
but in the wrong direction. Thousands of children today count down before
they count up, thanks to television and the space age. But don't worry. In
the long run he will have a better concept of numbers than earlier generations had, for today's kindergartner learns that numbers really have no right
or wrong direction. What is important is understanding their meaning and
knowing how to use them.

The essence of math teaching today is that instead of teaching rote
memorization and mechanical skills, it teaches your child to look for and
find quantitative meanings, relationships, and patterns. Quantity is all around
the kindergartner, in age, time, and space. Before he has learned to think in
an abstract way about quantity, he copes with numbers of chairs or blocks
and he has an idea of "a lot" or "a few" and of "more" or "less" and
"big" and "little" and "half" or "part of" something; but his ideas of
quantity are vague and unclarified. Chances are that if you give him a choice
between four one-inch pieces of a chocolate bar and one six-inch piece, he
will choose the group of small pieces. Thus, the purpose of his learning
experiences in mathematics in the first year of school is to extend his number
concepts and to help him to find quantitative meanings.

Math is a vocabulary.

Your child needs a vocabulary for thinking about mathematical ideas and for expressing them. In any kindergarten, this vocabulary will include adjectives such as "small," "short," "wide," "narrow," "long," and "few," with their comparatives and superlatives, plus other descriptives such as "part," "little," "more," "less," "half," "some," "all," "piece," and "whole." Geometric shapes, such as circle, triangle, square, and rectangle, as well as coins, will be included. In addition, in some kindergartens today, the language of mathematics is used in an easy and natural way, so that from the very beginning of his formal learning experience your child hears and handles such words as "number," "cardinal number," "ordinal number," "zero," "numeral," "one-to-one," "line segment," and "interior or exterior region of a circle or closed curve," Symbols such as + (plus), − (minus), = (equals), ≠ (is not equal), 0 through 9 (numerals), > (greater than), and < (less than) are common parlance.

There are two interesting sidelights about the teaching of mathematics today. First, in many schools no paper and pencil are used in kindergarten math. If your child attends such a school, all his learning experiences in number concepts will be oral experiences. On the other hand, he may be in a school where even in kindergarten the formalized workbook is a cherished institution. Second, in many schools no particular sequence of mathematical events is set up. In such a school, your child will study many concepts simultaneously, whereas in a more formalized system he will probably learn sets of five after he has learned sets of four, and subtraction after addition.

One method is not necessarily better than another, and often the method is dictated by the teacher's evaluating what preschool experiences the children have had in counting and identifying number symbols and geometric shapes, coins, and measures, as well as in quantitative thinking. What is important is that she take advantage of the countless daily opportunities, in other learning experiences, to include experiences with number concepts and that she lead your child through steps of reasoning that help him to begin thinking logically.

Number concepts out of cooking and carpentry.

What exactly are the gains your child will make in number concepts during this first year of school? What are the values he will derive? By the end of the year he will be able to count rationally and to recognize ordinal position. He will recognize likenesses and differences in size, shape, and positions of objects and will use the correct vocabulary to express comparisons. He will understand the concept of one-to-one correspondence (one for each, the same number as, or enough to go around) and will associate the correct numeral with sets of its corresponding number (a set is any designated collection or group of things). He will recognize, reproduce, and originate repetitive patterns. He will also develop an awareness of time in general and will recognize the hour on the clock.

The experiences through which these abilities are developed rise naturally out of such activities as cooking, carpentry, block building, and sewing and out of such classroom routines as attendance taking, snack time, and milk-money collection. They come, too, from games and activities which are planned and created for the purpose. However, the game that becomes a drill is a dangerous one. It leads to boredom and fatigue and the dislike and distaste with which mathematics has often been regarded. When that happens, one of the chief values of learning—its fun—is gone.

No teacher expects every child to master every one of these skills with the same speed—and neither should you expect them to. These concepts are reintroduced, and reinforced, in first grade because it is known that not every five- or six-year-old masters every skill by the end of kindergarten.

Mention should be made of the fact that the "new math" movement of a few years ago did some damage. Many youngsters were not taught computational skills—their math facts and "times tables"—without which they cannot do arithmetical computation.

Learning to count.

Your child will sing counting songs in school, probably in dramatized form with body movement or dancing. Such songs are introductions to rote counting in the old-fashioned way. They put the cardinal numbers in order and teach the number names. Rational counting, or counting by enumeration, comes next. This is the process of matching a set of objects with an ordered set of names for the counting numbers—that is, one-to-one correspondence. It is how a five-year-old finds out how many cookies are on the plate or how many people are in the room. He soon learns that there must be one object for each ordered number name. At first, the objects must be visible and should be tangible. Counting cookies or people has to come before counting days of the week or the age of a birthday child or the number of sounds played on a musical instrument, all of which soon follow. In fact, tangibility is quite valuable. When he first discovers rational counting, your child will probably start touching everything he counts. The next step is to point at everything he counts. Soon he will stop pointing and be able to count "in his head" and just by looking, and shortly thereafter he will be able to recognize numbers in sets up to five or so without counting at all. Right before your eyes, as the year goes along, he will have gone from a simple concrete conception to a complex abstract one.

Reading numbers.

Together with rational counting comes the learning of number symbols. This, of course, is reading. It establishes the concept that numerals are names for numbers. Many games, devices, and related learning experiences are used. The walk-on number line is one. It connects rational counting and number symbols graphically and establishes an important concept that will be used in math for a long time to come. In addition, your child will learn to respond orally to flash cards held up by the teacher, each one showing a quantity of objects (five strawberries or three kittens or four balls) with its number symbol. He will play with numeral cards, matching them to the number line on the floor, putting them in order after he has closed his eyes while another child mixes them up, putting them into empty spaces when a row from 0 through 9 has been set up with several omissions. Over and over again, the numerals on the clock, the calendar, and the pages of books will be pointed out to him.

Every five-year-old wants to be "first" or "next," so every experience of getting in line or taking turns gives him an opportunity to learn the ordinal numbers, or numbers in serial. Climbing the playground slide, getting snack-time milk, looking through a magnifying glass during a science experience—in almost everything he does, your child will hear the teacher tell him he is first, second, third, fourth, or fifth. She will ask him to bring the fourth book from the third shelf, or to take something to the second classroom on the left down the hall. Thus the serial meaning of numbers, which is as important to an understanding of the fundamental processes of arithmetic as the quantitative meaning, will become established.

What's it worth?

The concept of coins and money values develops out of the concept of counting and number symbols. After your child has learned to identify coins, they may be grouped in sets. Ultimately a set of five pennies will be seen to equal a nickel, a set of ten will equal a dime, a nickel and five pennies will equal a dime, two nickels will equal a dime, and so on. It is not expected that all these combinations will be learned at once. Emphasis is put on awareness of them and a grasp of the concept. A number of experiences will help your child grasp the value of money, a concept that is often quite vague. Kindergartners have been heard to opine, during dramatic play, that a dollar is enough pay for a day's work or that one hundred dollars is the going price for a sack of potatoes. A picture book of "Things I Would Like to Have" may show a lollipop on the nickel page, a balloon on the dime page, a popsicle on the quarter or even on the fifty-cent page, and a toy truck on the dollar page. When your child refuses to trade his newly purchased crayons for a classmate's candy, his concept of money values has won out over his sweet tooth.

Size, shape, and position.

Another concept that is basic to future work in mathematics lies in the recognition of likenesses and differences in the size, shape, and position of objects. Hiding games early in the first year of school will include putting objects in, beside, behind, in front of, and on top of a box. The relative heights of classmates, of furniture, of buildings will be compared. Graham crackers will be divided into halves and quarters and matched again. Objects will be lined up according to size from smallest to largest or largest to smallest. Cans, boxes, and balls will be compared for differences and similarities in shape. The aim is toward classification and identification of simple geometric shapes. As he sorts out objects by size and shape and learns to recognize geometric forms, your child will also learn that it is the edge of a circle that is the circle and the edge of a square that is the square. A plate is not a circle, and a box or book is not a rectangle, and his teacher will be careful to say that each is shaped *like* a circle or rectangle. She will illustrate the concept of a point by making a dot on the chalk board, and will demonstrate how two dots can be connected by many lines, straight, curved, short, or long. She will also indicate that a line may go on forever by drawing it with arrows at each end,

$$\longleftrightarrow$$

as she probably drew the number line when she first talked about it. She will encourage your child to recognize repetitive patterns in clothes and decorations and things he is doing with creative materials, to repeat them, and to originate repetitive patterns himself.

Time has position, too.

Relationships in time develop from the routine progression of the day's events as well as from counting and number symbol experiences. The idea that after snack time comes rest may be related to the idea that they are the fifth and sixth events on the day's schedule or to the idea that snack time comes when both hands of the clock are on ten, and that rest time will come when the big hand has moved along to twelve. The classroom is sure to include both a large, functioning clock and one or more toy clocks which can be manipulated by the pupils themselves, and work with creative materials will produce wrist watches, grandfather clocks, kitchen and cuckoo clocks, and clocks modeled from plasticine. Calendars may also be made from plywood or tagboard, with squares numbered from one to thirty-one to be put in place each day.

So many kinds of measurements.

Like so many other learning experiences, measurements keep bobbing up all over the classroom. Time is measured by the clock and the calendar and recorded in holidays and birthdays and weather diaries. Weight is measured and compared on scales and balances during free play with blocks or clay and during science experiments. Amounts are measured in simple cooking demonstrations. Linear measure enters into planning at the workbench and in maintaining records of pupils' heights on a strip of paper on the wall. Temperature is measured and recorded in the weather diary and in science demonstrations.

There is so much concrete learning in the area of science and mathematics that you might jump to the conclusion that your child will almost automatically become aware of the generalities involved. Don't kid yourself, or him. One of his most difficult learning experiences, and one of his teacher's most difficult teaching problems, is to bridge the gap between the concrete and the abstract.

A way to bridge that gap was found in the New York class that studied the supermarket. When they were comparing family size and composition, their teacher used progressive stages to introduce them to the bar graph. She began by having the children sort themselves into groups. Those who belonged to families having two adults and one child went into one group, those with two adults and two children into another group, and so on. Then simple one-line stick figures were drawn on the chalk board to represent each type of family, and each child made an x beside the type to which he belonged. On another day they cut out paper figures to represent each type of family, and the children stood in groups before the cutouts. They soon realized they could not stand there forever, and agreed that it would be good to put something instead of themselves before each figure. Blocks seemed most practical, and now a pile of blocks before each cutout represented the number of children who belonged to each family type. The blocks were counted and recounted and checked against the chalk-board tallies made earlier. After a few days, however, the blocks began to be in the way and were needed for other play, and so a flannel board was introduced. Flannel cutouts abstracted the figures and blocks in a flat, two-dimensional way, and shortly the children discovered one of the teacher's helpers drawing a bar graph with crayons. Several of the curious guessed that the long and short lines represented adults and children in family groups, that the bars in the graph represented the flannel blocks, the three-dimensional blocks, and the children themselves, and that the numerals to which the bars reached indicated the number of children of each family type. Finally, along came a student teacher who had not been in on any of the development. Using very much the same terms, each of several children explained the bar graph to her sensibly and understandably. They had grasped the logic of symbolizing quantitative information.

7

Experiences Involving Music

"I would teach children in grammar school how to compose music," says philosopher Eric Hoffer. "There is no reason you can't teach a child of six or seven to compose. If you can teach them to read, you ought to be able to teach them to read music. By the time a child is twelve, I should whistle something and he should be able to write it down."

Hoffer may have something there. Music is one of the languages of life. As an infant, your child probably heard song shortly after he first heard the spoken tongue, and music has been all around him (if not assaulting him) ever since, through all kinds of media. Therefore it will seem natural to him to find that music is an integral part of the day's activities in school.

An interest in music is natural.

He need not be a Mozart. Every normal child has a natural interest in rhythm and musical tone. Some have more tautly tuned inborn senses of pitch, of time, and of intensity than others, but all benefit from a variety of experiences in music and respond to opportunities to express themselves in some form of music.

The benefits or values of experiences in music in the first year of school are many. The chief one is the development of a stable attitude toward music as one of the pleasures of life. In other words, to put it negatively, your child's spontaneous love for music will not be inhibited. In addition, he will find his singing voice (if he has not already done so) and will discover that he enjoys songs as a means of expression. He will increase his awareness of sound and movement in his environment. He will learn to listen attentively to a song or short instrumental selection, to interpret the mood of music being sung or played, and to recognize fast and slow, loud and soft, high and low, long and short, and light and heavy in music. He will be able to interpret music freely through movement, recognizing and responding to rhythms such as walking, running, skipping, hopping, jumping, and whirling and turning. He will get to know the simple percussion and melody instruments, even making some of them himself, and will create simple songs and tunes. He will dramatize songs and listening selections, using percussion and melody instruments as sound effects.

Developing the singing skills.

In the kindergarten day, the music experiences are of several kinds. Some develop the singing skills. Probably half of the class comes to school able to sing a simple melody, having learned songs elsewhere, while others are shy and self-conscious and just want to listen at first. The five-year-old voice, contrary to popular opinion, is not especially high-pitched, though the shrieks it produces in spontaneous neighborhood play are exceptions to this rule. It ranges, on the average, from middle C to high C or D. The teacher's yardstick in selecting songs is the children's enjoyment, for songs are learned, not taught. She may conduct singing in a fairly formalized way at times, from the piano or, if she has a strong voice and a good ear, without accompaniment. Probably she will start off with familiar folk songs and nursery rhymes, such as "Skip to My Lou" and "The Farmer in the Dell." Length is no problem. Your child can easily learn a long song if he likes it and wants to learn it.

Rhythm but not drill.

The whole being responds to rhythm. Bodily movement in time to a beat is natural to children. It helps physical, emotional, and social development as large muscles are co-ordinated. Emotions are given release, and social development is encouraged by the group movement that occurs in dancing. Classroom experience with rhythm may begin in the first few days of school, with rhythm instruments for all hands, a recorded march, and a wildly disorganized parade of stomping and jingling individualists. It may, on the other hand, begin with the teacher at the piano finding and improvising simple rhythmic accompaniments for patterns created by the children, for basically it is the child rather than the music that determines the response. Few teachers today insist upon drill work in which the whole group makes the same rhythmic response at the same time to any given musical selection.

Creative and dynamic rhythmic activities will be encouraged, with tapping and clapping and arm swinging when the group is seated or in motion, and with varieties of running, skipping, walking, swaying, and swinging as the music calls for it. Many reliable old Mother Goose rhymes and folk songs (again, the dependable "Skip to My Lou") invite the listener or singer to act out the rhythm. Take, for instance,

>*Jack be nimble, Jack be quick,*
>*Jack jump over the candlestick.*
>
>*Right foot, left foot, any foot at all,*
>*Sally lost her pocketbook going to the ball.*
>
>*Ride a cockhorse to Banbury Cross,*
>*To see a fine lady upon a white horse.*
>
>*Ring-a-round-a roses, a pocket full of posies,*
>*Hush—hush—hush—we'll all tumble down.*
>
>*Hickory, dickory, sackory down!*
>*How many miles to Richmond town?*
>*Turn to the left and turn to the right,*
>*And you may get there by Saturday night.*
>
>*How many miles to Babylon?*
>*Three score miles and ten.*
>*Can I get there by candlelight?*
>*Yes, and back again!*
>*If your heels are nimble and light*
>*You may get there by candlelight.*
>
>*Wee Willie Winkie runs through the town,*
>*Upstairs and downstairs, in his nightgown.*
>
>*One foot up and one foot down,*
>*This is the way to London town.*

The repertory of skippable, danceable rhymes is endless.

Listening.

Hearing what the music calls for involves listening, and, as he gains experience in listening for rhythm, your child will discover length in music. He will begin to know how long a rhythm will last, and will be sensitive to the customary sixteen measures of many songs. His ear will become more acute in passive listening, too. From using some of them in class and from hearing solo parts, he will come to recognize the sounds of certain instruments. He will listen for beat and will begin to distinguish music that moves in twos or fours from that which moves in threes. He will listen critically in order to select suitable rhythm instruments for accompaniment. He will listen, also, to his own voice and to those of others for tone quality and pitch.

Instruments—classic or improvised.

Quite an array of rhythm and melody instruments can turn up in the kindergarten classroom. Swiss bells and wrist bells, triangles and tambourines, rhythm sticks, hand drums, cymbals, and maracas may keep the beat. Piano and autoharp, slide whistle and recorder or inexpensive tin flageolet, tuned flowerpot chimes, water glasses and bottles, or a xylophone may call the tune. While everybody will get a chance at everything, one time or another, the teacher is well aware that overstimulation and fatigue come quickly if every child uses an instrument at the same time. Probably she will have four or five use bells or melody instruments to accompany the singing of a lullaby or quiet folk song, or another small group beat out the rhythm for a march or Indian dance. Now and then a soloist will be asked to create the ticking of a clock with rhythm sticks or to play a special maraca and tambourine tempo for an original dance.

The creation of musical instruments is a valuable learning experience in which your child will discover the great variety of sounds that can be created from humble materials. Old chair rungs or sections of broom handle become rhythm sticks. Any number of bowls and cylinders—large cans, oatmeal boxes, cheese boxes—turn into drums when pieces of inner tube or of cloth, shellacked after it is drawn tight, are stretched across them. Long-necked bottles hanging from strings, filled with varying amounts of water, can be tuned to the scale. If the glass is clear, the water may be colored, and in the debate over which colors to use for which sounds your child and his class will gain a rich experience in analyzing the "feeling" of color that a high or low pitch generates.

Interpretation through music.

Whenever the subject of music comes up, the teacher will discuss the song or selection with the class, so that all can help decide how it should be used—sung or listened to or accompanied by rhythm or dramatized—to express a mood or idea. As they discover interpretation, the children learn to express themselves creatively. From here it is an easy leap to the creation of original songs, chants, and jingles that express the impressions they gain from field trips. The teacher writes down such songs and keeps them to be used and enjoyed again and again during the year. One class returned from a trip to an art gallery and, instead of writing a story, taped a song to the tune of "Loobie Loo" and accompanied on the autoharp. Each child took turns singing of what he had seen, and, if his phrases did not fit the matter at first try, he added or deleted words until it had rhythm. Thus, experiences in art and language were combined with those in music.

8

Experiences Involving Health, Safety, and Physical Education

Since for the five-year-old every experience is a learning experience, some rather routine facts that contribute to your child's expanding knowledge should be considered. When the teacher asks him to turn on the lights or open a window or adjust his chair to a better position at a table, she makes him aware of factors in good health. During the year, he will be weighed and measured, and his eyes and teeth will be checked. He will wash his hands before snack time and after using the toilet. He will learn that frequent changes in activity help him to relax, the quiet work at a table or on the floor follows strenuous activity indoors or out, that he takes off outdoor clothing when he comes indoors.

If your school is a relatively new one with a lavatory or two in each classroom, don't be surprised when you discover that boys and girls both use the same facilities and usually cannot be bothered to close the door. At this age, most of them couldn't care less. When they go to the bathroom, their minds are not on modesty but on getting back as quickly as possible to whatever they have interrupted.

Awareness of health.

Does the teacher still line up the kids for health inspection? No. Those days are mostly past. She can observe runny noses, coughs, signs of skin irritation, or other symptoms that need medical attention during the greeting and free-play period that starts the day, and she will refer to the school nurse any youngster who looks as if he might better have stayed home. If a number of children are absent with colds or something else, she will probably lead some class discussion about symptoms and remedies, pointing out the need to stay home and get extra rest during illness, encouraging the concept of medical treatment, and discussing the doctor's role. When a major medical discovery or achievement hits the front page or the television news, she will incorporate it into the learning experience of current events. She will invite discussion about growing big, when members of the class are weighed and measured. When farming and gardening are studied, she will include information about nutrition.

Cleanliness does count.

No matter where you live, your child will have one or more classmates who come to school dirty. Washing hands and face may be the first thing some children have to do in the kindergarten classroom, and they may need direct help in this real learning experience. Not everybody in the room will notice, but if your child is aware that the teacher has taken someone to the lavatory to get cleaned up he will have added a certain amount of experience about cleanliness to his store of knowledge. Of course, some kindergartners consistently manage to get dirtier than others during the first half of their day and need a good scrubbing before every snack time.

Safety.

Your child will be made aware of safety factors. If he pops marbles or jacks into his mouth or runs with sticks or tools or scissors, he will be warned of the dangers of such habits. He will experience a fire drill soon after school begins, and no doubt a visiting fireman will tell the class about the dangers of experimenting or playing with matches, guns, or wiring and electrical equipment. Experiences in the language arts and with creative materials will help to describe and depict safety rules and habits.

Games for basic movement.

Many physical education teachers are inclined to overemphasize the idea that the foundation for future basketball and football is laid in kindergarten with tossing beanbags and games of tag. Kindergarten teachers are more interested in the basic movements that are exercised and the perceptual abilities that improve as large muscles develop their co-ordination. In addition, social, emotional, and psychological behavior that may not appear in the classroom often comes out here. Character is built and personality developed in games and self-testing activities. Skills that will be useful in leisure time are developed, too.

Your five-year-old will not be forced into highly competitive games or impossible tests, but he will begin to learn the correct forms in such basic activities as running, jumping, hopping, skipping, throwing, catching, and tagging. He will learn the value of competing with himself in order to improve his performance and of various activities in improving his strength, agility, speed, balance, co-ordination, and endurance.

Rhythm experiences, such as those involving music, may take place in the school cafeteria, in the gym, or on the playground. Square dancing, for instance, and dramatization, in which the children play like giants or elephants or cowboys, offer large, free movment. Games involving beanbag or ball give experience in playing as members of a group and taking turns, and in the fundamental skills of throwing, catching, running, and tagging. The rabbit hop and individual or group rope jumping have calisthenic benefits in the large muscles. Walking a beam or log, hopping on one foot ten times, bouncing a ball, or skinning the cat on the monkey bars are self-testing activities that practice skills which will be needed in future athletics.

9

Experiences with the Unit Approach

It has been mentioned several times that learning experiences are seldom isolated. Often, however, the teacher tries to relate experiences among several subject areas in ways that are more than merely incidental. Such relating is known in the teaching profession as the "unit approach" or as developing a work unit in an area of interest. A unit lasts about two weeks, and you hear about it at home when your child (if he chooses to divulge what is going on at school) tells you day after day about Indians or the circus.

While the unit approach has been established for some time, it can be overdone. Teachers have recently been warned by their professors in teaching colleges that unit topics often are too big and complex and succeed each other too quickly. The danger seems to lie in too much concern with the unit itself and not enough concern with the long-range goal or total learning experience that lies beyond it. If it's the circus this week and Indians the next week and the zoo the week after, the residual learning may be all clowns and feathers and tigers rather than the concept of a cultural or natural phenomenon.

The planned work unit.

What happens in the course of a work unit? Take the study of the police and safety as it has been conducted in kindergarten in Grosse Point, Michigan. In art and creative work, the children make stop-and-go hand signals in red and green, paper police hats, murals of streets and houses, large street signs on broomstick posts, scrapbooks and bulletin boards for displaying cutouts, and drawings of police and traffic and safety situations. Games include "Lost Child," in which the children win turns at being the police officer by correctly giving their names and addresses, and "Where Is My Child?" in which the teacher describes her lost child to the police officer, who must find the child, as well as active games in which some pupils are police officers and others are pedestrians or drivers. Music activities include songs about crossing the street and traffic lights, rhythms which imitate mounted police, and singing games. Discussions which exercise the language arts go into the police and their work and how we can help them, safety rules and street patrols, add-on stories about police work, picture stories based on a cutout or drawing, and dramatizations of the police at work. A number of books from the school library or brought from home are read, poems are recited, and audiovisual aids—from the felt board to films and filmstrips—add to the picture. Finally, a field trip takes the class to a police station, a policeman or policewoman, crossing guard, or safety patrol leader (or all three) comes into the classroom and gives a safety talk, and a program is presented for parents or another class to show what has been learned about the police and our safety.

You can imagine the same sort of approach in a work unit on Indians, parks, or pets. When a class has been through several such units, it is able to cope with one on an abstract subject such as sound or on a more complex area such as the total school environment or a harbor.

The spontaneous work unit.

What is perhaps the most worth-while kind of unit or activity arises spontaneously. One of these began in San Francisco, when the children in Edith Van Orden's kindergarten at the Redding School noticed some spots on the leaves of a young avocado tree which was growing in their classroom. A few days later they saw holes in the leaves and worms eating the leaves. They began discussing what was happening and dug up information to explain what they observed. The teacher offered to keep a diary, as they dictated it, of their observations and related activities. They interpreted their observations and learnings with illustrations, dictated individual stories about the experience to the teacher, and put in correct sequence a series of flannel-board pictures illustrating the life cycle of the inch worm.

The diary itself will give you an idea of what happened during this experience, which combined science, language, and some mathematics:

Nov. 5

We saw tiny gold spots on the leaves of the avocado tree.

Nov. 13

We found holes in all the leaves.

We found caterpillarlike worms eating the leaves.

The gold spots must have been eggs. We think the worms grew out of these eggs. We think they are inch worms because they inch their way along.

Nov. 20

We have seen the inch worms spin a thread and drop down from a leaf as they spin it.

If we touch the inch worm he pulls in his thread which takes him back to the leaf.

Nov. 26

All that was left of the avocado tree was the stem and branches.

The inch worms were gone. We knew they had eaten all the leaves.

Maybe they were looking for more food.

We started looking for the inch worms.

John found one on the floor. He picked it up. It spun a thread and dropped down from his arm.

We found another one on Tommie's back.

We have only three inch worms now. We have them in a box with avocado leaves.

Dec. 3

We put the three inch worms in a jar and fed them avocado leaves. We have to feed them every day.

Dec. 10

We found one big fat inch worm on the side of the jar with threads spun all around him.

The avocado tree didn't die because leaves have started to grow again.

Dec. 14

We found the second big fat inch worm.

The third inch worm is still tiny.

Jan. 2

The first inch worm has turned yellow inside his cocoon.

The second inch worm is starting to make his cocoon.

Our avocado tree has many new leaves.

Jan. 4

The second fat inch worm has stopped making his cocoon.

We think he is not ready to change from his larval stage to the pupal stage.

We cannot find him.

Jan. 8

We found the second inch worm in his larval stage on the ivy plant.

John saw a brown moth in the jar. We don't know where he came from.

Then John saw something flying. It has a thin body, two wings, two feelers, and six legs. We don't know where it came from. We know that it is an insect because it has six legs.

Jan. 10

The second inch worm is back to the cocoon it started to spin and is spinning again.

The first inch worm that is in the pupal stage in the cocoon is beginning to look like a moth.

Jan. 11

Russell found another moth.

We know it is the first inch worm because his cocoon is empty. He has changed from the pupal stage to a moth.

The second inch worm is changing from his larval stage to the pupal stage inside the cocoon he finished yesterday.

Jan. 14

We found gold spots on the jar.

We know they are inch-worm eggs.

The two moths have laid them.

If the eggs hatch we will have lots of inch worms again.

If we give them avocado leaves to eat they will grow fat.

When they are fat they will be in the larval stage getting ready to spin a cocoon.

When they are in the cocoon they will change to the pupal stage and come out changed as moths.

Then the moths will start laying eggs again.

We found an empty cocoon. Now we know that the moth that John discovered came out of it.

The cocoon is in a leaf on the bottom of the jar.

We can't find the flying insect. We think it has died.

Jan. 22

We had a surprise today.

The inch worms hatched out of the eggs.

There are many, many inch worms in the jar and some have gotten out through the cloth.

They are so tiny we can hardly see them. They look like this.

They are trying to find food.

Feb. 4

There was a moth in the jar today.

The cocoon is empty. The moth is finished with the pupal stage.

The inch worms have eaten many of the avocado leaves. They are getting large.

Feb. 5

We watched the moth lay eggs.

We can see three fat inch worms on the avocado tree. Most of the leaves have been eaten.

We put another avocado tree next to it so they will have enough to eat.

We took a little tiny inch worm out of the jar and put it on the avocado tree.

Feb. 11

The leaves of the avocado trees were all eaten this week end.

The inch worms are all gone. We can't find them.

We did find a little one on the jar.

We brought in our last avocado tree for him to eat.

The moth has died.

Mrs. Tyner found one fat inch worm on the floor after school. She put him on the avocado tree.

Feb. 13

We found an inch worm on the Bulletin Board.

Miss Van Orden found a fat inch worm on the floor.

We hope they both stay on the avocado tree.

Feb. 15

We can find only one inch worm.

He is in the larval stage.

He is spinning his threads between the four leaves to make a cocoon.

We can still see him between the four leaves.

He hasn't changed to the pupal stage yet.

Feb. 18

All the leaves have been eaten from the avocado tree.

The lost inch worm must have eaten them because the inch worm isn't eating now.

We found the lost inch worm on the flower pot. There is nothing left for him to eat.

Feb. 18 (later)

Now we have another avocado tree. We are so happy.

Ricky Won from Room 11 brought us his avocado tree.

The inch worm is on the bottom of one of the leaves. He is this big.

A world of skills involved.

From this diary, you can see that a number of learning skills were exercised between November 5 and February 18. First came the observation skills. Through sensory perception, the children observed the spots on the leaves, the holes, the worms eating leaves, the fat worm that spun threads and then turned yellow inside his cocoon. They made certain assumptions concerning their observations, such as that the gold spots must have been eggs and that something was eating the leaves. They made predictions based on their observations and previous experience: If the eggs hatch, we will have more worms; if they are fed avocado leaves, they will grow fat, spin cocoons, change from larval to pupal stage, and come out as moths to start laying eggs again. Finally, they made conclusions, based on observation, which summarized the entire life cycle of the inch worm.

At the same time, listening skills were exercised. The children listened purposefully, paying close attention to such comment as John's observation that he saw something with a thin body, two wings, two feelers, and six legs and to the teacher's reading of reference sources which described insects so that they could compare the descriptions with the creatures they had found. They listened critically, in order to detect flaws or errors in their assumptions or conclusions and to note points that might not be in proper sequence.

Oral language skills.

Discussion of the inch worms gave experience in oral language skills. The class had to recognize the importance of maintaining orderly procedures in their group discussion. They learned, as well, to conclude a discussion by summarizing the main ideas, by drawing appropriate conclusions and generalizations, and by posing problems for further consideration—as when they found more gold spots on the leaves, decided they must be inch worms, too, and agreed that if they hatched there would be more inch worms and the class would have to get more leaves for them to eat. At the same time, in their oral reporting, they had the experiences of translating their observations into words, of clarifying and refining their statements, and of dictating sentences to record their observations. They organized their ideas orally into proper sequence, stating their inferences and assumptions and selecting pertinent observations to back up their inferences. They had to connect their observations with causes and reject inferences or assumptions which they discovered to be false, and they had to select the right words to convey their meaning and express their ideas clearly and concisely, stating their conclusions with appropriate reasons.

The inch-worm study exercised reading skills, too. It helped the five-year-old to understand and appreciate the function of reading, encouraging him to approach the act of reading with confidence and, as he helped prepare the printed record of an interesting experience, to recognize that reading conveys ideas. Moreover, reading comprehension developed as the children supplied correct words and phrases, formulated a concept by applying a definition ("We know that it is an insect because it has six legs"), and understood the sequence of ideas that made up the life cycle of the inch worm.

Writing skills.

Skills in written expression were also enhanced by the inch-worm experience. The need for recording the entire experience was understood. The information to be recorded was selected. Furthermore, the type of writing was suited to the material: The diary was the best way to record day-by-day observations and activities, and the individual stories were suited to expressing individual reactions to the study.

Thinking skills.

Finally, certain mathematical thinking skills were effected. A feeling for the passing of time was generated by the observation of the life cycle. Dates were read, discussed, and referred to. Mathematical language was used: Inch worms "inch" their way along and get larger; trees and worms and leaves were observed in sets; cardinal numbering counted three trees, three worms, four leaves, six legs; ordinal numbering counted first worm, second worm, and third worm.

Out of this extended learning experience came not only the concept of the life cycle in nature but certain appreciations. The sound and feeling and connotation of words were relished by the class. The children experienced the fascination which nature holds for the close observer. They took pride in the special skills and contributions of classmates, such as John's power to observe. They found, also, the introduction to reading and compositional writing to be a pleasureable experience.

Part Four

As the Year Goes On

The novelty of going to school soon wears off. The routine remains. As the days go by and you become aware of what specific learning experience is occurring, you may be anxious to know how you can continue to help your child at home.

You can help by keeping in mind the learning experiences that your child will have, watching and listening for signs or news that they are going on, and supporting them with daily experiences at home and in the community. This does *not* mean that you should attempt to teach reading, writing, arithmetic, or any other school subject, although you can include your child in simple arithmetical calculations with measuring cup or spoon, with change making and cash-register tape, and with linear measurements at the workbench. You can continue to provide creative materials and encourage their use, to comment on science in daily living and on current events, to go places and do things other than routine.

You can help, furthermore, in three specific ways: first, by continuing to understand your child's needs in the areas of play, habits, and health; second, by understanding his teacher's background and her role in evaluating his progress; and third, by understanding the "readiness" with which he will move successfully into first or second grade. The following chapters will discuss each of these ways.

1

Play, Habits, and Health

Everybody needs privacy now and then. Children especially need to know that both a private time and a private place are always available to them. Time shared with no one is essential to creativity, to remembering what happened in school, to projecting what might have happened, to daydreaming, and to just thinking.

The importance of privacy.

A place in which your child can be alone is equally important; it need not be an entire room, though a room of his own with a door that shuts is ideal. It can be a corner of a room or even a corner of a table. What is important is that it be a place in which privacy is respected, where an uncompleted project can wait to be worked on or a group of dolls or toys can wait in suspended animation from the last game. The place should have a decent light and some kind of box or container in which private possessions may be stored; it should be reasonably quiet. Quiet is an essential element of the private time and the private place. If there is to be the opposite of quiet— noise, chatter, singsong, conversation, radio, TV, records, or tape—let it come from the owner of that private time and place.

Your child's concept of the self was discussed earlier. This involves his

97

freedom to be and the way in which freedom and choice enable him to take charge of his life. Having a private time when he wants it, and a private place, are vital to his developing concept of self. Also vital is something that develops out of the continuing school experience and the continuing availability of private time and place at home: the continuing need for an audience. "See the fort I built" or "Watch me dance" or "Look at the picture I drew" or "Listen while I sing" or "We're going to put on a play"—all are invitations for an audience. But note that the audience should always be an invited one, for sometimes an audience is the last thing your child wants. If he has a tremendously complicated imaginative game going on, in which blocks create streets and buildings and stuffed animals ride on toy cars and trucks, and he has not invited you to watch or comment, you will be wise to keep out.

Help when asked, but not more than asked.

Help is also something he will ask for when he needs it. If you step in to umpire the game or correct the tune or mix the paint or make the costumes unasked, you will only spoil the fun. When you are asked, on the other hand, do what you are asked and let it go at that. If the green paint is all gone and you are invited to solve the problem, demonstrate the mixing of blue and yellow but don't expatiate on pointillism or Picasso. When your child asks for help or an opinion, he builds his self-confidence. When he receives aid or advice unasked, it subtracts from his self-confidence.

Toward mental and emotional well-being.

Mental growth, as noted earlier, is a patterning process. One part of the pattern is the development of conscience. A good conscience is like a good parent in that it controls the behavior of the person of whom it is in charge. Using knowledge and understanding and logic, conscience considers the proposed behavior—or that which has already occurred—in the light of the values and requirements of social environment. You can help develop it by talking things out with your child. From time to time he may try out all kinds of unacceptable behavior, including using bad language, being late, and various forms of deceit from lying and stealing to cheating. He may express such behavior because of emotional distress and unhappiness rising out of the lack of some essential needs, such as attention and affection and opportunites for achievement and success. He will not yet know the difference between right and wrong in all cases, even though he may have learned by now the distinction between true and not true. Often when a grownup accuses or scolds him, he denies doing something or lies to cover up. Your willingness to talk things over and listen with understanding will be far more effective in helping him to develop conscience than all the shame, suspicion, and scolding you can summon. Moreover, your care in setting rules that are practical and possible to follow and then enforcing them consistently, just as the school environment sets and enforces its rules, will help you avoid creating situations from which guilt feelings may arise.

Feelings.

Feelings are funny things. Sometimes they come right out, and sometimes they stay hidden. The expression of anger is, within limits, a healthy thing for your five-year-old. If he suppresses his anger, it may show itself in nervous tension. By engaging him in any kind of vigorous play or workout when you find feelings of anger pent up in him, you can help provide a constructive outlet.

Feelings of *fear* are often less overtly expressed than anger. With his vivid imagination and his habit of learning through his senses, your five-year-old may be subject to any number of unreasonable or unfounded fears, ranging from traffic to dogs, based on limited experience with a minor auto accident or a large, unruly pooch. Verbalization about his fears is difficult for him. Probably he does not even understand his fears, and he may be afraid to admit that he has them. Doing something constructive about his fears is the best way to help him. One way is for him to act out or play out fears by dramatizing them with toys or dolls or in games. Another is for you to pause with him and observe the cause of the fear, noting how much traffic moves without accident or how other children play with a dog. It will not be helpful for you to joke about his fears or shame him for them or try to get him to do something brave when he is unsure of himself. The "you're a big boy now" approach lays the basis for a coverup and for not looking at the cause of the fear. You can help establish a basis for sound mental health by admitting candidly that everyone, including grownups, has fears.

Be ready for timidity.

Timidity is a form of fear, and may show up in the first school experience. The teacher will help all to feel secure during the first few days of school by previewing the day's schedule, so that everyone knows what is going to happen and when it will be time to go home. She also helps the security of all in such ways as making sure that furnishings and supplies are always kept in the same places and can be found easily. If a child is hesitant about joining in, if he sits alone at a table and watches the others or keeps himself preoccupied at his cubby, she will find ways to make him feel important and needed. You can do the same thing at home, by discussing things that are going to happen, by not making major or abrupt changes in the home environment during the early weeks of school, by finding ways to make your child feel important and needed.

Toward social well-being.

You can help your child's social growth in many ways and among people of many different ages. At this age, his friendships are often brief and intense, and they should be encouraged. If he talks of a particular school-mate or two, you might ask him if he would like to have the friend come over to play. Remember that he probably plays in a small group during the free-play period first thing in school each day and that very likely the composition of the group as well as his friendships shifts from time to time. Such changes of allegiance are signs of widening interests and growing maturity. He may have outgrown one child to discover a mutual interest in another.

Belonging to other groups.

As he begins to sense his membership in the kindergarten class, you will probably find that he is increasingly aware of his membership in other social groups, whether his own family or a neighborhood gang or your church. Look for opportunities to reinforce his impression of his acceptance and approval by the group, remembering the three A's that he needs—acceptance, approval, and affection. At the same time, he has certain re-sponsibilities to the group. One is that of not keeping others waiting. Kin-dergarten teachers, realizing how difficult it is for a five-year-old to interrupt an absorbing activity, warn their pupils a few minutes before they are expected to go elsewhere or to do something else. In the same way, you can help the habit of promptness to form by issuing warnings about time for bed or for going out. Remember also that youngsters vary in the speed of their motor controls and reactions to stimuli. If you demand immediate action—toys put away, bedclothes put on, hands washed—without warning or time for your child to react or finish what he is doing, you may edge him toward nervousness that can become extreme.

How to cope with quarreling.

Quarreling is also a matter of responsibility to the group. Kindergarten-age children often get rid of their tensions almost in unison through quarrel-ing, simply because they may never have been required to discharge them in any other way. Often it arises because the children themselves do not know how to handle a social situation. You can step in with a constructive solu-tion, suggesting a game in which an object that caused the quarrel may be shared, or diverting attention from the individual whose nose is out of joint. It helps if you can kindle some laughter in the process.

Set the example.

The best way to develop basic kindness in your child is by example. Courtesy and acts of friendliness are learned no other way, and, since "please" and "thank you" and consideration for others will be exercised in the classroom, it is important for them to be echoed around the house. Thoughtfulness will be shown by the teacher and class in extending a warm welcome to the child who has been ill or a farewell party to one who is moving away. When you are sending flowers or writing a note, you can give your child a learning experience in thoughtfulness by including him in an active way, in the trip to the florist or in signing his name.

The teacher will also be encouraging consideration for the possessions and property of others. Pride in the appearance of the classroom, "a place for everything," and respect for the care of materials all need to be reinforced at home. Just as the teacher will consult the children for solutions to problems involving the care and organization of possessions and property, so can you often include your child in such problems at home. Remember that, in his private place—his room or corner or table—possessions that seem insignificant to you may be precious to him.

During the first year of school your youngster will probably meet a greater cross section of religious and racial groups, and of physical, social, political, and economic differences, than he has ever known before. His emerging awareness of social strata will develop not only from meeting his classmates and working with them but from many of his social-studies experiences as he learns about his community and the world beyond the schoolhouse. At home and away from home, you can influence his concept of the dignity of the individual and his acceptance of human likenesses and differences by the values you set on elements such as status and possessions, or on physical attributes and handicaps.

Toward physical well-being.

Early in this book it was stated that at the age of five your child's rate of growth is slowing down. It is continuing, however, and, generally speaking, it is controlled by two factors: heredity and environment. It is already too late for you to do anything about the first. You can continue during the coming year to do something about the second. Environment includes all the physical and psychological elements outside your child's body—food, sleep, health, family, and social life.

Records of height and weight will be kept at the school, and you can keep them at home as well. Their value lies not in comparing them with anybody else's record. Your child is growing at his own particular pace. There is no right or wrong height or weight for him at any age, and he is likely to reach plateaus at which he shows for a time very little increase in size. Usually, a growth spurt follows such a plateau. The record is useful only for showing when and to what extent growth has occurred in the individual. To compare it with the record of an older brother or sister or neighbor or classmate may only cause needless worry.

Some facts about growth.

Certain facts are known about growth patterns. All other things being equal, large adults were large children. (This does not mean that *all* large children become large adults.) Children who are maturing more rapidly than others the same age will be taller than the others. In the primary years of school, children who are physically more mature are the better students, apparently because of differences in motor and manipulative abilities more than any other factor. Girls (again, generally speaking) are more mature than boys and perform better than boys the same age. So you can help your child's image of himself as this first year of school goes along by keeping these factors in mind and, as you get to know his classmates, by watching for the early achiever, the rapid grower, the big boy (not merely the over-weight boy), and the average-sized girl—any one of whom may be your own child. Thus, if your child is the girl who is too tall or is ahead of her classmates and feels too different, or the slight, late-maturing boy who is unable to match some of his pals in physical co-ordination and achievement, you can talk sensibly about it and point out that no two human beings grow at the same rate.

Too much stimulation or an emotional upset before going to bed are likely to affect sound sleep. The result is poor adjustment in school. The teacher spots a listless and inattentive pupil and knows he is at a disadvantage. You can help by setting regular times for going to bed and getting up, by giving ample warning of bedtime, and by avoiding overstimulation just before bedtime. Never associate bed with punishment.

Good posture is a sign of good general and mental health, while often (but not always) bad posture is a sign of a problem that cannot be solved merely by saying "stand up straight" or "sit up straight." If your child's teacher notices consistently bad posture, she will probably suggest that you seek help for him through the school physician or your family doctor. The problem may be caused by poor diet, ill-fitting clothing or shoes, lack of fresh air and exercise, sleeping on a poor mattress, or playing and working at a table that is badly lighted or the wrong height. Generally speaking, your child's posture is symptomatic of his sense of self or lack of sense of self.

You don't want to make a little hypochondriac of your child, but it is a good idea to give him an unobtrusive daily health checkup. You can do it while asking him if he has washed his face and hands and if he has a clean handkerchief or tissues. Look for skin eruptions and skin coloring (cold or bluish skin may indicate poor circulation or poor nutrition) and for dull or watering eyes, pale lips, general listlessness, or irritability. You will proba-bly hear about a sore throat before you look for it, and coughs and sneezes will announce themselves. It hardly seems necessary to say that such symptoms call for keeping the child at home for treatment, but every teacher at every grade level can tell you about children who were sent to school when they "should have stood in bed."

In Appendix B you will find a list of common childhood diseases, with their symptoms and the usual duration of time lost from school.

Continuing help in observing, listening, and speaking.

Knowing something about the countless learning experiences that are going on in school will guide you in helping your child increase his observational, listening, and speaking skills at home and thus in helping him get ready for reading.

Keep up games of observation. "What do you see that is green?" "How many red cars?" "Is that house a split level or a ranch?" Try comparison games. "Which is taller?" "Sweeter?" "Colder?" "Heavier?" In the store, let him find items from your shopping list. At home, encourage his painting and modeling and block building in its symbolic and realistic stages. Let him dictate stories to you, encouraging his powers of description. Continue to go places where you can see things that are not routine for him—the zoo, the airport, the farmers' market, the museum or art gallery.

You can make reading a part of daily living in numerous ways. Books and magazines in the home, especially those published for your five-year-old, with a bookcase or section of bookcase for his very own, are important. If you can, see that the house contains a good encyclopedia and a good dictionary, and use them with your child. Make frequent trips to the library, and let him have and use his own card and find books that interest him. Finally, probably nothing is more important than reading aloud to him.

Keep talking and praising.

Conversation adds words to his speaking vocabulary, and the more vocabulary you use and he uses in conversation, the better off he will be when he starts reading later on. Encourage him to talk about what he has seen and done, and give him your full attention when he talks. Your attentive listening makes him feel that what he has to say is important. Include him in discussions of family plans, whether you are discussing what to have for dinner or where to go for vacation. Give him every opportunity to verbalize his thoughts and feelings and observations and to hear others verbalize theirs.

Praise for the child is like fertilizer in the garden; he will grow and thrive on it. What might be an easy victory or a small success to you may be a giant one to him. Let him know when he has done something well, and let others know, too. Talking about him to others outside the family is a way of showing that your laurel wreaths are not bestowed only in private.

Your interest in his school will influence your child's attitude toward it. This not only means listening as he talks about school activities (but don't grill him); it also means seeing the teacher regularly for conferences and participating in parent organizations and special programs. If you can serve as a "room mother" or "room father," that's ideal. You will get to know teacher, school, and class.

When parents and educators are partners.

In some schools, you may have an opportunity for direct involvement in helping to create a more effective learning environment for your child. California's Early Childhood Education Program, begun under the direction of state superintendent of public education Wilson Riles, has established a policy that literally calls for the participation of parents in program planning, program implementation, and program evaluation and modification at the local school level, grade by grade.

The California law (Education Code 6445.01) states:

Parent participation shall be included in a manner which:
(a) Involves parents in the formal education of their children directly in the classroom and through the decision-making process of the California school system;
(b) Maximizes the opportunity for teaches and parents to cooperatively develop the learning process and its subject matter. This opportunity shall be a continuous permanent process;
(c) Recognizes that the continuity between the early childhood education program and the home is essential.

The code also establishes that the adult/pupil ratio in the classroom shall be approximately one adult to every 10 pupils, and calls for the use of aides, volunteers, and parents (whom we must also assume to be volunteers) to achieve this ratio. This opens the door for every parent who is concerned about what goes on in the classroom to become deeply involved. The result is that in at least some California elementary schools you can find almost as many adults as pupils. And you will find individual school plans written for the children of the particular school by parents and members of the school staffs.

Is the program successful? Apparently. San Diego, for example, reports higher test scores, more enthusiastic attitudes about school, and less pupil absenteeism than before the program began.

2

The Teacher

Ideally, the kindergarten teacher is a learner, a guide and counselor, and a humanitarian. She must learn, from the first day of school, the stage of development that has been reached by your child and some forty to fifty others (assuming she teaches, as most do, two daily classes of twenty to twenty-five). She is constantly augmenting her professional and cultural background and increasing her understanding of child development. She is a guide and counselor, who must be sensitive to and perceptive of the problems and the needs of five-year-olds individually and in groups. She is a humanitarian, who has a love of teaching and of fun and who loves and respects young children.

Is the kindergarten teacher made in Heaven and handed down? You might hope so, for she is the person who is destined to guide your child in one of the greatest adjustments he will make in his lifetime—that from home to school. As he breaks from the first security he has known into a series of new surroundings and conditions, she lays the foundation for all his future learning.

Her training and resourcefulness.

Again ideally, the education and experience that have brought your child's kindergarten teacher to his classroom are of a special kind that has emphasized developmental learning and the understanding of children. She is a graduate of an accredited four-year college, with major work in early elementary education completed at the graduate or the postgraduate level. She has taken special courses in human growth and development and has studied the interrelationships of school, parent, home, and community. She has also studied and absorbed the history and philosophy of education, as well as its current problems.

Her task: to interpret your child's individuality.

Perhaps the single most important benefit that she gets out of all this background and continuing training is her respect for human personality and individuality. She understands the common bonds of humanity and knows that the similarities in general outweigh the differences among children. Racial, social, and economic differences do not interfere with the opportunity she gives her children. Her task is to interpret the child's individuality and give it the best possible chance to grow and find itself.

Her basic knowledge of child development means that she understands how your child grows, thinks, behaves, and learns. It means evaluating each phase of his growth and accepting him at his present stage of development. Your child may be more active than others and find it harder to sit still even for brief periods. He may be more persistent and find it hard to end one activity when it is time for another. He may be more distractible and find it harder to pay attention to his work. He may need more reaction time than another, which means he never quite gets his hand up or his word in before someone else. He may warm up slowly, needing more time than others to get used to a new adult, new routines, and strange children. By understanding and accepting whatever stage he is in, his teacher can understand his needs and move him forward according to his own rate and level of development.

Her stamina and stability.

It takes plenty of physical stamina to be a teacher at this level, and it takes emotional stability and a special kind of poise, too. Robust good health, the ability to withstand cold weather during playground times, the nimbleness and agility to bend and squat to the child's level on a moment's notice a thousand times a day, manual dexterity with all the creative materials in use, a pleasing voice, good peripheral vision, acute hearing, and the ability to appear neat and attractive are physical requirements. At the same time, while quickness of movement and alertness of mind are necessary, it is important that the teacher not be tense and jumpy or move too abruptly. Her controlled calm and authority and her self-confidence must be established and maintained in the classroom regardless of accident, illness, unacceptable behavior, or just plain mess. Moreover, she is lost without a sense of humor.

Not every kindergarten teacher would agree with John Holt, author of the penetrating book, *How Children Learn,* when he says that the teacher's role is to "give children as much help and guidance as they need and ask for, listen respectfully when they feel like talking, and then get out of the way." But the best teacher follows this precept. She watches for clues to your child's needs and supports his efforts by answering his questions and guiding his play so that it challenges the capacities she has discovered in him.

Her teaching techniques.

Teaching techniques have many aspects. They include orienting the child to the school and its work by stressing "we" and "our" in all projects in which the entire class takes part. They also include knowing how to develop good feelings between teacher and child by being enthusiastic and human and how to earn respect by being consistent and fair and by talking neither down to nor beyond the child. The technique of assuring orderly behavior includes maintaining a businesslike atmosphere in the classroom, with promptness in getting to work and quiet during rest period or listening time and helping the children to sense the difference between play and rowdiness, humor and silliness, and disagreement and quarreling.

The kindergarten teacher organizes her schoolroom with forethought, planning the activity areas and quiet areas to balance each other, setting definite places for materials, making seating arrangements functional and flexible. At the same time, she knows the importance of keeping the room attractive, with centers of interest and beauty spots and with displays mounted interestingly and colorfully—and changed frequently. She recognizes the necessity for certain distractions—such as trips to the bathroom and the untangling of chairs and arms and legs—but works to keep them to a minimum. She knows that good relations between parents and school will further the child's learning and that her cumulative records of the child's development will be helpful to those who teach him in future years.

Her role in evaluation.

Your child's teacher begins evaluating his work on the first day of school. What is evaluated? His capacity for original thinking, his ways of working with others, his ability to find alternate ways to solve problems, his use of skills appropriate to his stage of development, his methods of handling materials and of following through on plans, his improvement in attitude, his honest effort, and finally the results that satisfy the pupil himself.

These elements are evaluated by a combination of methods. Certain information about him is kept in cumulative records. It includes his home and family background, data on his health, weight, height, and growth, notes on his social behavior and interaction with his classmates and adults, his recurring patterns of behavior, his dislikes and avoidances, his achievements, potentials, and interests, and his apparent feelings about himself and other people.

The teacher gets this information from preschool registration and conferences and home visits with you, from her day-to-day observations and accounts of what your child does and says in given situations, from diaries and examinations, and from the observations of other school staff members. She jots down her observations on language ability, social and emotional adjustment, and maturity in growth almost daily.

From her records she is able to evaluate the progress of the group and of your child's individual achievement in relation to the group, as well as his individual growth and development in relation to those the same age. At the same time, she is evaluating her own teaching methods and technique. She keeps a check list of your child's habits of work, his knowledge of safety rules and school rules, and his basic motor and perceptual skills such as walking the balancing board or recognizing colors and sounds. She records the progress of the creative work of each child. She keeps a class chart on which names are recorded as accomplishments show up. Group progress is recorded on charts to show experience with songs or dancing, stories or picture books, field trips or work units.

Frequent self-evaluation is vital to your child's growth. It encourages his initiative and builds his self-confidence, lets him find satisfaction in his own progress, and develops an appreciation of the progress of the group. Self-evaluation is encouraged when the teacher, circulating through the classroom during a work period, asks him what he thinks is the best part of the work he is doing or if it is better than what he did yesterday or if he can do better next time. It is again encouraged when she interrupts the work period to draw everyone's attention to a good job that is being done or to say, "What would you like to tell us about your work?"

Her conferences with you.

Hardly any parents merely "send their children off" to their first school experience. They go with them, often actually and always psychologically. Your child's teacher will be aware of this fact, and may invite you to stay in the classroom the first day or the first several days if it seems necessary in order for your child to accept the idea of being there. She and the entire school staff look upon the work of home and school as a single co-operative undertaking and hope that you can each share the skills and understandings of the other. With her understanding in depth of all five-year-olds, she offers you a chance for greater understanding of your child and how he grows and learns and why he behaves as he does. On the other hand, with your understanding in depth of your particular five-year-old, you offer her a chance for greater understanding of what makes this individual tick. Her work with him can be much more effective if she knows what out-of-school experiences he has had and is having.

Report cards are rare.

Formal report cards with marks are rare in most kindergartens—and in many primary grades as well. You find out how your child is doing in a private conference with his teacher. This will come after the first month or six weeks of school, and again whenever you or the teacher feels the need for a conference. She may have prepared an informal report card (known in many school systems as a "Conference Form"), but this is mainly for the purpose of guiding her conversation, or at least providing a point of departure for the conversation. Probably this form has two sections. The first is headed, "Personal and Social Growth," and lists a number of items marked either "Excellent," "Good," or "Needs Improvement." Some schools hesitate, in the kindergarten year, even to differentiate between "excellent" and "good." They mark these items only if your child needs improvement. (Some schools use a more comprehensive, detailed form than others. For an example, see Appendix A.) Areas of personal and social development are likely to include the following items:

HEALTHFUL LIVING
    Practices good health habits.
    Observes safety rules.
PERSONAL DEVELOPMENT
    Plays well with others.
    Respects rights of others.
    Observes rules and regulations.
    Shows growth in self-control.
    Accepts responsibility.
    Displays positive attitudes.
    Shows an eagerness to learn.
WORK HABITS AND ATTITUDES
    Follows directions.
    Completes work begun.
    Works well independently.
    Works well with others.
    Takes proper care of materials.
    Develops listening skills.
    Practices neatness.
    Participates in group discussion.

The second page is headed, "Growth in Learning and Skills" or "Scholastic Achievement and Effort." Again, a mark for either "Excellent," "Good," or "Needs Improvement" may be given for achievement as well as for effort. The areas reported probably include:

LANGUAGE ARTS
    Shares ideas and experiences with others.
    Expresses ideas clearly.

Responds well to stories and poetry.
Is a good listener.
MATHEMATICS
Uses numbers with understanding.
Understands math concepts.
Reasons well in solving problems.
Is acquiring number facts.
SOCIAL STUDIES
Understands concepts.
Secures and uses information.
SCIENCE
Understands concepts.
Secures and uses information.

Your child shows special interest in areas marked:

Arts and Crafts	Science
Music	Social Studies
Stories and Poetry	Physical Education

The conference is, in fact, a discussion, an interchange of views. This is a time for an exchange not only of information but of feelings. If you have gotten to know and have confidence in the teacher and if you are worried about some aspect of school or of your child's behavior, you may want to let the teacher in on it. She may be able to provide the reason you have been looking for, or what you have to say may give her the reason for some behavior in school that she has wondered about. Her records of your child's perceptions and of anecdotes about him may help you to see growth and emerging interests and new behavior that you have not recognized. Often, you are so close to your child that you cannot see small but important indications of growth and learning.

The important thing to keep in mind is that your child is being marked for his ability for the task. Some parents think their child should be marked against other children. The best teachers, who have worked hard to know each child's capability well, mark the child against himself.

Share your information.

A few things should be remembered about conferences with your child's teacher. It is usually wise to share information about your child with his kindergarten teacher; however, unless there is a professional necessity, which you and she agree upon, for including the information in his record or for consulting the school principal or guidance counselor, information of a personal nature about your child or family should go no further. You will be wise to keep other children, brothers and sisters, neighbors or classmates, out of the discussion. The teacher will expect you to take the initiative in solving problems; she has not taken over your job as parent. Nor should you expect her to interpret the entire curriculum in one short conference; you are there to discuss your child's progress.

What about I.Q.?

A word about the I.Q. (Intelligence Quotient). Psychologists agree that the kindergarten year is too early for testing the I.Q. In fact, not all schools test even in first grade. Some wait until second or third grade. Some now make it their policy to give no group I.Q. tests in any grade level. Furthermore, there is more than one reliable test. And finally, no single test is definitive. Different children respond differently to different tests at different ages. Yet every principal has met the parent who "just knows" her five-year-old has a "genius I.Q." When your child moves beyond kindergarten, you'll find that most teachers simply do not get into discussions of the results of I.Q. tests. Most principals do, though they often prefer to say only that the I.Q. is high, average, or low. However, in most states, parents may now exercise their right to know precisely what the school has determined about the I.Q.

Parents at school.

In most schools, you are welcome; that is the most important thing to know. You are welcome—any time. Drop in and say hello to your child and his class if you are in or near the building. Go for the day and observe the entire session (but do say you are coming beforehand, lest too many parents turn up simultaneously). Accept the invitations that ask you to come around, for they are extended with real enthusiasm.

You may receive many such invitations. A fall tea, at which you can get acquainted with the parents of your child's classmates, may be held. Education Week may provide a planned program that demonstrates something going on in class and includes displays and dramatizations. The PA or PTA (Parent Association or Parent-Teacher Association) is sure to invite you to its meetings, which are usually held in the evening so that both parents can attend; at least one of these usually includes a visit to the classroom and an informal discussion by the teacher about what is going on. Meeting night, incidentally, is *not* the time to get your child's teacher into a detailed discussion of his particular progress or problems.

Are you a 'resource person'?

A personal invitation may ask you to come to school as a "resource person." If you are a parent who has built a lifelong collection of dolls from all over the world, or who has a loom and does his or her own weaving, or who is a puppeteer and can show how to make and use puppets, you can make a valuable contribution to the curriculum. If you are a father or mother who is a dentist or who manages a store or who is a musician, you can be equally helpful. Professions, businesses, hobbies, travel experiences, special talents—all can become learning experiences when parents come to talk about or demonstrate them.

Often, such resource persons are found by Key Mothers (sometimes Key Fathers now, too). They are parents who help in a number of ways—organizing committees and activities; supplying materials such as large cans, boxes, cartons, and old shirts; cutting, fitting, and sewing costumes; chauffeuring on field trips or riding in the school bus. Those who have learned the ropes this year may help out during preschool registration come spring and summer. Other helpers are Room Mothers (again, or Fathers), who bring treats, assist at birthday parties and on special holidays, and send snacks for milk time (if school policy permits).

The P.T.A.

Nearly every school has a parent organization—either a parent association (PA) or a parent-teacher association (PTA). Many PTAs belong to the National Congress of Parents and Teachers, which has branches in every state, chapters in thousands of localities, and units in many more thousands of schools. Other PAs or PTAs unite in federations in their own school districts or affiliate with well-established organizations in their own localities, such as the Public Education Association and United Parents Association in New York City.

The objectives of parent organizations are what you would expect: to promote the welfare of children and youth, to raise the standards of home and school life, to secure adequate laws for the care and protection of children and youth, to effect close relations and co-operation between parents and teachers, school administration, and school boards, to develop united efforts between educators and the general public—and at the same time to monitor school programs and "watchdog" when and where the schools may be taking a wrong turn.

Most parent organiztions have a variety of publications for their members and the public. The Congress, for example, publishes a monthly magazine, a monthly bulletin, and a large number of paperbound books and pamphlets on subjects ranging from mental health to good reading for parents, from extremist groups to evaluating TV programs, from mass media to juvenile delinquency. In many places you can join a preschool PA or PTA before your child goes to school. The PA or PTA will be a functional part of your relationship with his school throughout the next twelve or thirteen years.

In many communities, the placid days of old, when parents accepted the school as is, have long been over. Financial, behavioral, achievement, and in some instances racial problems have focused public attention on schools all across the nation. In addition to the organizations already mentioned, new ones, like the National Committee for Citizens in Education, based in Columbia, Maryland, are educating parents and the public on such questions as the rights of students, parents, and the handicapped, public access to information and records, the significance of declining reading and math levels, accountability of teachers and supervisors, and a host of other major education issues. Many of these questions will probably be new to you as the parent of a kindergartner, and no one will expect you to know much about them at the start. You will find, however, that very few PAs and PTAs these days operate in the old style of bake sales and teacher helpers with galoshes and supplies. If you're interested, you'll probably get as much of an education about school issues and problems as your kindergartner will get about growing and learning. In the process, you may wind up not only finding ways to help your own child but also the larger community of children in your locality.

3

Moving Up

Is he ready for first grade?

What is readiness? When is readiness?

Life would be so simple if only June 1 could be declared National Readiness Day and if all five-year-olds who are going on six could be passed through a grading and testing machine and either stamped with a purple mark that says "U.S. Approved READY" or sent back for reprocessing.

It would also be so dull.

Since no two children are exactly alike and no two schools are exactly alike, we can hardly expect readiness to be the same in all cases. Yet there are always parents somewhere who expect readiness to arrive with the robins in the spring and who walk into the classroom and say to the teacher, "Are you going to do readiness now?"

Readiness, we said many pages ago, is that stage in a child's physical, mental, emotional, social, and empirical development when he is able to undertake a given learning experience with ease, understanding, and interest. For a given learning experience there must be a given readiness or more than one kind of readiness, and so there are: general readiness for a variety of formal learning experiences (as distinguished from the more informal learning experiences of the kindergarten), communications skills or language arts readiness for reading, numerical readiness for mathematics, and handwriting readiness.

General readiness.

Knowing that he will have to manage certain academic tasks in first grade, your child's teacher watches, as the kindergarten year draws to a close, for signs that he is ready for the expected tasks. In effect, she is measuring or evaluating his level of maturity against his calendar age and the levels of maturity of his classmates.

The signs are many. He is in good physical health, free from defects in sight, sound, speech, or large muscle development. He understands his home, school, and community, and has explored these environments widely and gained a broad background of experience in them. He has made a good adjustment to school, understands the routines, can work independently some of the time, is free from feelings of fear, failure, or undue pressure, and can work without social or emotional difficulty with other children and adults in small groups. He has developed his vocabulary and usage well enough to help plan, discuss, and share experiences, and is able to describe objects and events and tell stories. He can listen attentively for more than just a few minutes at a time. He knows how to use creative materials, from crayons and paper to clay and paints, reasonably well. He can listen to, understand, and carry out instructions and suggestions, and assume some responsibilities with them. He is independent of home and parents enough to enter wholeheartedly into school activities. Of course, not every kindergartner exhibits every one of these achievements by the close of the year, but most exhibit most of them and are ready to move up.

Reading readiness.

Readiness for the communications skills includes all the foregoing signs plus the basic perceptual skills. There are many signs or characteristics here, too. Though many of them are, in fact, interdependent and inseparable, it's more practical to discuss them somewhat individually as visual, auditory, and speech characteristics.

The signs that your child is *visually* ready for reading include his interest in books, signs, and captions—that is, in the concept that words and symbols in printed material convey messages and tell stories. He discriminates visually in perceiving likenesses and differences in objects and in simple symbolic forms. He identifies positions and directions in spatial relationships and recognizes the common colors. This familiarity with visual direction and orientation brings him easily to the eye and hand movements of reading—the left to right, top to bottom, and front to back progressions—while his discrimination between symbolic forms brings him the ability to learn the letters of the alphabet and to perceive word forms. His eye and muscle development is mature enough for him to "sit and focus" on reading charts and cards without eyestrain (despite the fact that probably he is still rather farsighted).

Listening readiness.

At the same time, he shows signs of auditory or listening readiness. The relationship between listening and reading is vital: A beginner will read no better than he listens. His auditory discrimination includes the ability to hear likenesses and differences in letter and word sounds and in word beginnings and endings, to follow a series of ideas in their proper sequence, to enjoy games and activities involving word sounds, and to enjoy stories, poems, and descriptions read aloud to him.

The speech characteristics that indicate readiness to begin reading are tied in closely with the visual and auditory characteristics. For instance, when your child is ready, he is able not only to follow a series of ideas in their proper sequence but to retell and re-explain them to others. He can hear part of a story and predict an outcome and can complete an unfinished sentence with words that make sense. He speaks in complete sentences and can tell an experience or story in sequence. He can report to a group (not necessarily the entire class, but a small group) without getting rattled and with order and sense in his narration, and in such speaking or reporting, as well as in private conversation, he uses a variety of expression. He has good pronunciation and enunciation, and can match spoken phonic sounds.

Whether or not some actual practice in reading is introduced along in April or May of the kindergarten year depends on a combination of factors: the school, the teacher, and the particular group in the kindergarten room. Some school systems make it a matter of curriculum practice to start reading before first grade, and some do not. Some teachers find their kindergarten group on the whole so "ready" that it would be a mistake to hold off reading. Through her constant evaluation of your child, the teacher has a strong "feel" for his readiness and for that of the class as a whole. The best schools encourage the teacher to act accordingly.

Number readiness.

This stage of development, like the others, involves several aspects, each of which is really a mathematical concept. If he is ready for number work, your child understands the idea of counting and is able to count at least to ten. He recognizes one-to-one correspondence and number sets at least up to five. He grasps ordinals up to the fifth, too. He knows the simple geometric shapes and the simple units of measure in quantity, size, time, money, and distance. He understands relative value in money and relative size in geometric shapes. He has been up and down the number line. He can think in terms of quantity, and he has mastered a specific number vocabulary.

Handwriting readiness.

Though many children arrive in kindergarten already able, by rote memorization, to "write" their names, most teachers neither encourage nor discourage this particular skill during the first year of school. It is not, in itself, an indication of readiness for handwriting. Rather, as the year goes on, the teacher looks for signs that your child has developed well-rounded facility in the use of the small muscles of his hand and fingers and that a pattern of hand dominance has become established. As he works with paper and pencil or crayon, she watches for the co-ordination between eye and hand that develops from his easel painting, cutting, pasting, drawing, and modeling, as well as from games, dances, and rhythmic activity. He is ready when he has reached a stage of control in which he can make all the recognizable lines and circles which combine to form the manuscript alphabet and when he has become aware of the need for writing both compositions and names, labels and signs.

June has come, bringing with it the prospect of the next big year. As your schoolgoer turns six and heads for first grade, many of the characteristics that leveled off on a kind of plateau of growth and behavior at five suddenly spurt again. Physically, he may outrun his own capacity for fatigue, becoming exhausted before you or he knows it, in his active and boisterous day. Mentally, he is apt to jump to conclusions and to have difficulty making decisions, as he lives intensively in the present and is more interested in the activity than in its result. Socially, he is either high in the favor of his peers, or is highly disliked, and is a brash know-it-all who fights to be first in everything. Emotionally, he craves praise, is easily discouraged, fears lack of understanding, may play the buffoon, is ready to fight, but is also sensitive to his parents' and his teacher's needs, emotions, and tensions.

How much of this change results from his having had a year in school and from his having packed worlds and worlds of experience and wonderings and skills into his cranium? No one knows for sure. But it is a certainty that his experience and wonderings and skills, vast as they may seem from these pages of description, have only just begun. He is ready now for years of intensive and more formalized learning.

Part Five

Some Things to Think About

The very fact that children are starting school at younger and younger ages may be the salvation of schools in general, for school as we have always known it is an overloaded information machine. Because he has lived for several years in an environment overloaded with messages from media, the child comes to school already well stocked with information and ready to use all his senses in his learning.

A few years ago, many elementary educators saw great promise in the nongraded school. The idea of the nongraded school begins with the fact that nearly all children continuously grow and develop but that no two grow and develop at the same rate or in the same way at the same time. Therefore, why set calendar target dates for promotions to the next higher grade level, why force learning areas arbitrarily into grade levels at all, why not help the learner to advance at his own best speed along the continuum of language arts, the continuum of mathematics, the continuum of science? Under this system, the child covers a topic, but he covers it not because he has reached the fourth month of the third grade and the topic has bobbed up on schedule but because it carries him further in his continuing learning and understanding of the concept to which it belongs. In the process, the pupil assumes greater responsibility for his own learning.

Today, the nongraded school is not held in such high favor. Some teachers regret its decline in popularity and feel that the "back to basics" movement made it unacceptable. Others report that, while the nongraded program worked well for some children, it did not work best for most. One reason given is that those who start out in a nongraded school have trouble with routines when they move up into a graded school—such as most high schools.

In Chicago, a 'continuous progress' system.

The Chicago elementary schools, on the other hand, seem to have an established success in their Continuous Progress/Mastery Learning program. It is based on the philosophy that learning is a continuous process in which each child progresses to the next higher level by attaining mastery in various areas of learning at his own rate of growth, based on his level of experience, maturity, and readiness.

Chicago has removed grade designations. The curriculum is divided into learning levels through which the pupils can move upward without restrictions as to time, semester, or school year. Each level has its own standards for performance on established objectives which the students must reach and maintain. Children are grouped in the classroom according to their learning needs and are placed where they can develop best. The result, say Chicago experts, is both schools and classes organized for effective teaching and learning—and an individualized education for every child.

Many nongraded schools still call their first year "Kindergarten." Some have two-year sections called Kindergarten I and Kindergarten II and a Primary Unit, which may last three calendar years. But the student moves along to Kindergarten II or to the Primary Unit not when a prescribed number of months has passed but when his learning indicates he is ready. In the process, he has been launched into an atmosphere that permits real harmony among learner, subject matter, and the processes of learning, rather than into an atmosphere that sets up artificial barriers between them.

Don't hesitate to question.

Early in this book, it was stated that these pages would describe the typical kindergarten—a composite of those found in schools throughout the United States. While striving to give that *typical* picture, the book has also, in a sense, described the *ideal* kindergarten. Not every school or every teacher matches the description found here. If you find, unhappily, that your kindergarten and teacher do not match the ideal, you may want to go to your school principal and try to help work out improvements. Not every school is right about everything, and not every teacher or administrator is wise, and often parents can help to bring about changes that are needed.

At the same time, remember that you may have developed ideals or expectations about school programs that are beyond the abilities of children themselves. Many a parent arrives in the principal's office to demand a program that reflects an exaggerated idea of what his or her child can do. It is important to know which abilities the youngster has—the listening skills, the language skills, the ability to concentrate, *if* he has them (and by no means all have them)—and to let him learn how to use them.

In a word, do question. Do look closely. Know what is going on and what should be going on. Give your support or suggestions from as well informed a base as you can. And know your child.

All of which brings us to the point where, based upon the descriptive background of kindergarten, its pupils, and teachers that you have been reading, you may want to think about where your child is and where he is going. Where is he mentally, in terms of *thinking?* Where is he developmentally, in terms of physical, emotional, and social growth?

Kindergarten is where the world outside your home begins formally to help your child build the cognitive structures he needs to organize experiences to make sense out of what is otherwise incoherent and confusing. It is where your child begins to learn how to think in an organized way.

A word about Piaget.

Swiss psychologist Jean Piaget has earned a worldwide reputation by studying how your child's thinking process develops. He sees four stages that we may define simply as:

1. Lack of awareness. Until your child was about six months old, he didn't know that an object existed unless he could see it. If you took a toy out of sight, it ceased to exist for him.

2. Object constancy. After six months or so, your child thought out the fact that an object existed even if he could not see or touch it. If you showed him a toy, then put it behind you, he looked behind you.

3. Conservancy of mass or volume. It won't be until your child is anywhere from seven to eleven that he thoroughly understands the concept of mass or volume and sees that they are conserved in the same quantities no matter what shape or arrangement they are put in. Until then, for example, if he sees two differently shaped glasses of water containing the same amount, he thinks that the larger glass contains more liquid. Eventually he discovers that differing shapes can hold the same amount.

If you think about Piaget's simple illustration, you can apply it in countless directions. And you will understand that, until he crosses the invisible line into Piaget's third stage, your child will probably prefer to have five pennies rather than two dimes, or two small dips on his ice cream cone rather than one large dip—and will probably give you a blank look when you try to explain that $4 + 4 = 8$ is the same as $6 + 2 = 8$ and the same as $5 + 3$ or $2 + 2 + 2 + 2$ or 4×2 or 8×1. Coping with conservancy is a giant step in your child's mental ability.

4. Adult conceptualization. At about eleven, your child completes the acquisition of adult ideas of time, space, number and causality. He can deal with such abstract concepts as justice, government, or the themes of books.

No child, says Piaget, can be pushed or hurried from one of these stages to another. Each comes in due course, and your child must be prepared by experience for each major change. His mind lacks many abilities that adults take for granted, and these abilities must be learned before he can move along to the next stage. His teacher's role is to encourage him to find things out for himself and to challenge his thinking continuously by confronting him with conflicting evidence. That's why, when she finds him observing that a stone sinks to the bottom of a tub of water, she will have him try to sink a piece of wood the same size. You may call that play. The teacher will call it a science experience. Piaget calls it cognitive development.

Patterns of behavior.

There is another kind of development to think about. It has to do with the behavior of your child. Not whether your child is good or bad today or tomorrow, but broad general patterns of behavior.

The Gesell Institute in New Haven, Connecticut, has been studying the behavior of children for many years, originally one at a time and more recently in groups. You might think of the Gesell studies as diagnosing motor behavior in very specific ways, while Piaget studied cognitive behavior or the faculty of *knowing* in children.

What the Gesell people have found out is that behavior has patterns. There is four-year-old behavior. There is five-year-old behavior. And six-year-old behavior. But they do not necessarily come at exact chronological ages. Five-year-old behavior may not appear just when your child is five years old, because everybody develops on his own personal timetable. So the age of development that has been reached may be ahead of or behind the chronological age.

At Gesell, they've observed six different "cycles of development." These six stages keep coming around, repeating themselves from when your child is a tiny baby until he is about out of the teen-age years. Gesell labels them (1) smooth behavior, (2) breakup behavior, (3) sorting-out behavior, (4) inwardizing behavior, (5) expanding behavior, and (6) fitting-together behavior.

The following is a basic description of what goes on at each stage, showing the developmental age at which each of the six types of behavior occurs and briefly describing each stage, so that you can recognize it when it happens. A couple of key points to remember: There's nothing wrong with your child if he's as much as two years off the schedule, because growing times are different; when nothing seems to be happening, your child is just incubating between stages.

STAGE 1: SMOOTH BEHAVIOR.

Occurs at 4 weeks, 40 weeks, 2 years, 5 years, 10 years, and 16 years.
Look for your child to be steady, solid, not demanding of himself. Nothing rocks his boat. He likes to do what he's asked to do. Has a drive to be good and to co-operate.

STAGE 2: BREAKUP BEHAVIOR.

Occurs at 8 to 12 weeks, 2½ years, 5½ years, and 11 years.
Look for your child to recognize that things are not as he thought they were. He becomes aware of his limitations; so he starts opposing things. He needs routines and rituals.

STAGE 3: SORTING-OUT BEHAVIOR.

Occurs at 16 weeks, 3 years, 6 to 6½ years, and 12 years.
Look for your child to be unpredictable. Difficult one minute, not difficult the next. Generally he's easier to live with than during breakup behavior. He begins seeing solutions for problems.

STAGE 4: INWARDIZING BEHAVIOR.

Occurs at 20 weeks, 15 months, 3½ years, 7 years, and 13 years.
Look for your child to become withdrawn. You may become worried that there's something psychologically wrong. This is a time of fears, of difficulty with the whole outside world. Your child has a lot of *feeling* going on, and not so much action. This is when your three-year-old panics when you go out. Your seven-year-old writes with his nose pressed against the paper. No one understands your 13-year-old, for whom nothing is right and who has bad posture, mumbles all the time, listens constantly to music, and talks incessantly on the phone.

STAGE 5: EXPANDING BEHAVIOR.

Occurs at 18 months, 4 years, 8 years, and 14 years.
Look for your child to think the faster the better. In learning and doing, he is out of bounds and, you may think, out of control. Most of the walking harnesses are sold to parents whose toddlers are at the 18-month developmental stage—climbing, digging, pulling, darting, but with no sense of danger. Your 14-year-old boy will be picking on his father, even fighting him physically. On the other hand, your 14-year-old girl's expanding behavior may make her a top-notch candy-striper, and just great with the elderly.

STAGE 6: FITTING-TOGETHER BEHAVIOR.

Occurs at 2 weeks, 32 weeks, 21 months, 4½ years, 9 years, and 15 years.
Look for your child to establish equilibrium and see many ways to solve

problems. This gives him difficulty with choices and a lot of concern with reality versus nonreality. At 32 weeks, he's very fearful of doctors and relatives. At 21 months, everything is "mine." At four and a half, he gets a big kick out of being frightened by fantasy, then asks cautiously, "Is that really true?" At nine, he worries about school, about the state of the world, about the family budget. At 15, he "wants it like it really is" and expects you to practice what you preach.

Taking those stages in sequence and starting with your child at the developmental age of four, here is a composite picture of what to expect—as described by Miss Jacqueline Haines of the Gesell Institute. This quick picture will take you about five developmental years ahead with your child.

At four.

Starting at four—in developmental years, remember, not necessarily in actual years (your child may be older or younger)—the key phrase is "out of bounds," both in imagination and in motion. Your child is extremely active. He is learning through motion. Because he likes to be socially involved with other children, nursery school that is truly *nursery* school may be a good idea. The point to remember is that he is still self oriented—not group oriented. You still need to keep a sandbox outside where your four-year-old can play by himself.

At four and a half, youngsters start fitting things together. They are likely to become frightened by the very monsters they love. They're scared of the dark. They choose black to color with. They're concerned about death and mourning, probably without literal understanding.

Then at four and three-quarters, your child prefers to color with blues and purples. Still very active and mobile, he's excellent in nursery school—but don't let that fool you into thinking he ought to be in kindergarten right now. He may be starting to count well and use some big words, but he can't structure the language yet because he's only *just* putting it together. He's likely to reverse letters and numbers.

At five.

At five, he quiets down. He has good equilibrium. Doesn't want to get out of the house. Wants to cook and set the table. Seeks approval. "Can I do this now?" "Is this good?" Your five-year-old wants to get his authority from the adults. His mother is the center of his world.

Then comes five and a half. Along about February of the kindergarten year, he won't listen any more and won't follow directions. You may find yourself saying, "School has ruined my child." Now he's in disequilibrium. His motor is running like mad. His thoughts are always six steps ahead of himself. He has a number of health complaints. He tires easily. "My feet hurt," he says. He gets ear infections. He gets colds. All these are good reasons why he should not be pushed into first grade, for he cannot sustain a full day of school. In fact, if he's in first grade at a developmental five and a half, he will probably fall asleep every afternoon. If he's under too much stress, you may find him vomiting and having toilet accidents. This is also an age of discovery. He finds out he can cross his eyes. He may seem to have real visual trouble—getting the picture reversed, turning letters like B and D and G and Q into almost any other letters. The only thing to do about all this is wait patiently.

At six.

At six, some of this behavior remains. But he's sorting out. Now he becomes egocentric and aggressive. It's an age of action, not feeling. Six-year-olds keep tumbling out of their chairs in school. They're highly distractible. They can't seem to look you in the eye. They drive you crazy with endless talk. They're teething again—chewing on napkins, clothing, pencils, fingernails. They're clumsily falling all over themselves, catching all the contagious diseases, scared of bees and blood. Their motors are running so fast that they stutter. They have trouble telling the truth and taking blame. They get into arguments and power struggles. They may start stealing things. They thrive on praise, but you'll search hard for something to praise. They have trouble getting going to school in the morning, and then they can't leave school to go home. They have an eye fixation so that they lose their place in reading and have to use a finger running down the page.

At seven.

The calming-down comes at seven. Now your child may be withdrawn. He has trouble stopping things, needs time to finish any task. He's unhappy about recess coming if his worksheet is unfinished. His vision may be very focal—so he has trouble copying both from the blackboard and from a book. (This is the age when the nose comes down to the paper while he is writing.) He loves the pencil as a tool. Loves erasers. Likes to be read to, for now he's a good listener. Inner tensions, in this age of feeling rather than action, result from his taking in more than he gives out. And, right now, he's a great blackboard washer.

At eight.

At eight, he's healthier again and has plenty of energy. He likes praise, and is interested in how adults react to him. The eight-year-olds will furnish their own peer discipline. It's an exuberant, dramatic age—full of "wow" and "zowie!" Your child will now make a great third-grader—sociable, sports-loving, sharing ideas and conversation.

At nine.

At nine—another change. Now he's apprehensive. He's striving to become independent, but it's a task. He withdraws from the family circle.

There's no point in bossing him—he just resists it. He may shift his allegiance from Mom to someone else. He has a good relationship with his Dad. He's concerned about how well he does in school, and he functions well if he's left to himself. If you ask him about his teachers, they're either "wonderful" or "terrible."

At ten.

Then comes 10. Flexible, adaptable 10. It's a good age. Your word is law. And your child is the rock of Gibraltar.

What can you conclude from all this?

Primarily, you should be aware that your child's placement in a grade in school should be geared not to his chronological age but to his developmental age. Five-year-olds need an activity-oriented classroom. They need plenty of the outdoors. To enter kindergarten in September, a child should, ideally, be five by about June 1. Thus school systems should not admit any child who turns five later than July or August—yet many admit those who turn five as late as December 31.

If you have a boy and his birthday is in August, September, October, November, or December, you'll be smart to keep him at home—or in an activity-oriented nursery school—for another year. If you have a girl (girls, remember, develop earlier than boys) and her birthday is in November or December, keep her from kindergarten another year, too.

Because so many schools do accept children who really should be in prekindergarten with plenty of motor activity, most kindergarten teachers adapt the curriculum, especially in the early months of the year, to accommodate them. They know that if a child is behind developmentally and is pushed to bring his developmental age up to his chronological age, he may become a "surface learner" in order to get through. As one expert puts it, "It's not what we expose them to that counts—it's what they're ready to assimilate. Not until they're eight years old are they physically ready to handle reading, writing, and arithmetic. That's why the program before the age of six should be social—including kindergarten. Prenurseries and nursery schools *must* respect the physical organism of the child and not try to teach academics. Play is a child's way of learning. When we structure play, we interfere with learning."

What teachers and principals say.

Other teachers and elementary school principals say it in other ways—each giving you something to think about:

It is my opinion that each child is born with a defined potential and can reach that peak whether they start to read at three or at seven. Most children I've seen that have had parental pressure to read at an early age miss out on many of the early childhood stages that are prerequisites to any academic achievement. Many who are cheated out of their childhood often regress later on emotionally and/or socially. If we go with the child's internal time clock, we will get more evenly adjusted students.

A kindergarten teacher in a suburban school in Westchester County, New York

In this community, there is big status for the parent if the child is reading before kindergarten. They think that will determine the child's academic progress and determine the future. But what they don't realize is that the child will reach a plateau and then he won't *read no matter what you do. Reading is not just skill after skill. You're teaching reading so the child can learn more—whether it's baseball or astronomy. Now our Board of Education wants us to establish a vocabulary curriculum. But they don't realize that vocabulary is part of every curriculum—math, science, social studies. It's built into everything else.*

The principal of a New England elementary school

One parent told a first-grade teacher that her child was bored. The teacher said no child in this room can be bored—it's impossible for any six-year-old to be bored.

An elementary school principal

Let them be children. Let them play, talk, use their fingers, use their whole body. That's very important to the later intellect. But parents don't want to hear the word "play."

An elementary school principal

Parents are pushing their children to excel academically and to read at an earlier and earlier age. It's artificial; kids will read when they're ready to. The headstarts don't last; reading levels of accelerated and nonaccelerated kids usually end up about the same by sixth grade.

The director of a private elementary school.

Many parents still think that because a child learned his letters and numbers on Sesame Street he's ready to read in kindergarten. Very few are.

A California kindergarten teacher

These conclusions among teachers and principals are reinforced by those of Dr. David Elkind, a psychologist at the University of Rochester who started his own school in 1974 to deal with learning disabilities. His studies have led him to the conclusion that many who are labeled "learning disabled'' are actually suffering from what he calls "curriculum disabilities." They are, he says, handicapped by teaching methods, not by innate disabilities. He believes that reading instruction that begins too early, in first grade or before, may generate lifelong problems. The average child must reach the age of six and a half or seven before he gains the logical powers to understand the complexities of a word, such as the idea that a given letter has its own name and may have various sounds depending on the context. Reading lessons in kindergarten or first grade, he says, may be a trap that almost guarantees failure for many children. He urges putting off most formal reading lessons until second grade.

Dr. Elkind's conclusions are supported by a California kindergarten teacher who says, "I think we start many things too early for some kids. Not all are ready for workbooks, charts, and reading in books. But I'm afraid these things are here to stay."

Keep 'back to basics' in perspective.

They seem to be here to stay at least through the current vogue for going "back to basics" in reading, writing, and arithmetic. (Vogues do occur in education, as you'll discover as you follow your child through the school years. Many pendulums swing through public education.) Rote learning of multiplication tables is coming back. Adjectives and adverbs, nouns and verbs are being identified again after having disappeared in the "new English." But mathematical theory and writing composition must come with them if your child is to benefit.

Try to keep back-to-basics in perspective. One former teacher, who is now an executive with the National Education Association, says of parents who push back-to-basics: "They want us to make kids like they used to be, but parents don't want to be like parents used to be." In opinion studies, he notes, parents have revealed that while they care little for traditional values such as hard work and love of God, family, and country, they nevertheless want those values instilled in their children.

It's really a question of whether you're going to think about small objectives or large ones. Dr. Paul Brandwein, who has studied more than four thousand curricula in schools in this country and around the world, notes that the back-to-basics movement concentrates on small objectives and loses sight of larger ones. He finds children stifled by what he calls "drill and kill" curricula such as the step-by-step learning involved in math and language versus what he defines as intuitive, artistic, and moral ways of learning. He urges recognition of children's individual differences, permitting each to progress at his own speed. "There is nothing so unequal," he says, "as the equal treatment of unequals. Besides, what's the hurry? Perhaps when life spans were shorter, children had to learn to read when they were five—but now?"

Dr. Brandwein cites studies showing that an early start in reading makes very little difference: Children who are not taught reading until the fourth grade do just as well in a few years as those who were taught to read in kindergarten. More important than getting a child to read at an early age, he says, is allowing him to succeed. "To be cared for and loved," he concludes, "are the most important ingredients in education. Teaching is not a profession. It is a mercy. Schools are the one place where people can be human."

Appendices

Appendix A

Prekindergarten Registration Screening Forms and Kindergarten "Report Cards"

In some schools, a questionnaire like the following is used by kindergarten teachers and elementary school principals when they interview you and your child during registration, in the spring or summer before kindergarten.

The purpose is to let the teacher and principal know how the parent views the child, and to help prepare the teacher to cope with the child's levels of social, intellectual and physical maturity. For example, an only child who has not been to nursery school may need one kind of help from the teacher; a child with brothers and sisters, or one who has attended nursery school, has had a great deal of experience in group relationships and may have very different needs. Knowing that all learning is individual learning, the school is trying to find out how your child's learning style will be affected by the group process.

If you are concerned about starting the teacher off with preconceptions, or if you consider any question an invasion of privacy, you have a right to use your own judgment about answering.

1. Child's Name _____
2. Date of Birth _____ Date of Registration _____
3. Family Background
   Names and ages of other children in family:

Relationship of kindergartner to other children (attitudes)

Relationship to parents (attitudes as dependent, independent, one-parent oriented, etc.):

Occupation of father:
Occupation of mother:
4. Neighborhood Play
   Does child prefer to play alone? With playmates?
   Age of close friends:
   In neighborhood play, is child a leader? A follower?
5. Previous School Experiences
   Nursery School: Length of time child attended?
      His/her reaction:
      Other?
6. Health
   Allergies: foods, bites, etc?
   Handicaps: physical, speech, other?
   Does child have any strong fears or anxieties? Explain.
   Note any additional health information that might be of help to the teacher in working with your child.
7. Hand preference
8. Does your child have access to
   a) scissors
   b) crayons
   c) other art material
9. Personality of Child
   Reaction to a new situation:
   Can child wait his turn, or is he impatient and easily upset?
   What would you say is the *one* predominant personality trait characteristic of your child?
10. Interests, Skills, or Responsibilities
    Child's main interest:
    Special skills:
    Responsibilities of child at home (clean up room, etc.):
    Is child dependable at home?
11. What do you hope for your child to gain from his kindergarten experience?

NOTE: All of the above information is confidential, and will be used only for the purpose of becoming better acquainted with your child. Thank you for your time and cooperation.

   Check below as it applies to your child:
Will ride bus   _____
Will walk home   _____
Will be picked up   _____

Some schools check your child during registration by using what they call a "Prekindergarten Screening." This is *not* a test. It is a device to help the school determine which physical, social, and language skills your child has already developed. On a check list, the teacher or principal who is registering your child will mark whether he is, for each of the following developmental tasks, at the appropriate age, below the age expectancy, or over the age expectancy.

The Gross Motor tasks, for example, help to tell the teacher how well developed your child's laterality is and whether he is left- or right-handed. The Cognitive Verbal tasks help find out how well developed his listening skills are and whether he understands directions. The Fine Motor tasks also indicate handedness and small-muscle skills.

In some states and school systems, screening procedures have become tests in an atmosphere in which the child, in unfamiliar surroundings, does not do well. You are entitled to be aware of such testing methods, and you are entitled to refuse to permit their results to become part of your child's cumulative school record. Early observation of your child in the classroom can give the teacher much the same information as the screening gives.

The following is a typical check list:

Developmental Tasks
I. Gross Motor
    A. Hop on one foot four times in place.
    B. Skip four steps.
    C. Balance on each foot alternately with eyes open for 10 seconds. Do same task with eyes closed for four seconds.
    D. Walk three yards on toes without touching heels to floor.
    E. Walk backward three steps.
    F. Catch a large ball at a distance of six feet.
    G. Throw a tennis ball a distance of six feet—with right hand, with left hand.
    H. Sight on fixed object through rolled paper—with right eye, with left eye.
II. Cognitive Verbal
    A. Count 1 to 20. [Observer notes numerals and order.]
    B. Reproduce model. [Observer builds three steps with six blocks, then asks child to do the same six inches from model.]
    C. Count objects. [Observer places three blocks on table and asks child how many blocks there are.]
    D. Identify color: Red, white, blue, black, green, yellow.
    E. Recognize and name five or more letters on a printed page of large type.
    F. Read a short sentence.

III. Fine Motor
   A. Reproduce folded-paper model. [Observer folds 6- by 6-inch paper diagonally, then folds it in half. Hands child another piece of paper to fold like model.]
   B. Touch thumbs to four fingers on both hands.
   C. Copy letters D, N, E from model. [Observer does not demonstrate.]
   D. Cut four-inch circle with scissors to within one-eighth of an inch of the line—with right hand, with left hand.
   E. Color four-inch square within the lines—with right hand, with left hand.

In addition to checking your child's ability to handle these developmental tasks, the screening may include language and speech checks, such as those on the following list:

Language and Speech
   A. Assessment of Child's Language Comprehension
      _____ Below Average _____ Average _____ Superior
   B. Auditory Sequential Memory: Digit Span

1. 9 - 1	___ ___	8. 8 - 2 - 9 - 3	___ ___
2. 7 - 9	___ ___	9. 1 - 6 - 8 - 5	___ ___
3. 8 - 1 - 1	___ ___	10. 4 - 7 - 3 - 9 - 9	___ ___
4. 6 - 4 - 9	___ ___	11. 6 - 1 - 4 - 2 - 8	___ ___
5. 5 - 2 - 8	___ ___	12. 1 - 5 - 2 - 9 - 6	___ ___
6. 2 - 7 - 3 - 3	___ ___	13. 7 - 3 - 1 - 8 - 4	___ ___
7. 6 - 3 - 5 - 1	___ ___	14. 5 - 9 - 6 - 2 - 7	___ ___

Score ____   Age Level _____

   C. Analogies
      1. "A hat goes on your head. Shoes go on your _____."
      2. "Fire is hot. Ice is _____."
      3. "Milk is white. Butter is _____."
      4. "When you are *asleep,* your eyes are _____."
         "When you are *awake,* your eyes are _____."
   D. Story Sequencing (copy verbatim what child says).
      _____ Below Average _____ Average _____ Superior
   E. Same-Different: (use circle-square and car-truck pictures)
      "Which one is not the same as the others?"
      "Which picture is not like the others?"
      1. _____
      2. _____
   F. Why
      1. "Why do you take a bath?"
      2. "Why do we have clocks?"

G. Articulation
   1. Voice
   2. Fluency
     [Observer gives series of sounds and listens for child's ability to repeat them smoothly and with "liquidity" versus choppily.]
   3. Language
     [Observer gives series of words and listens for child to string them together as a sentence.]
H. Vocabulary
   1. orange   ———————
   2. envelope   ———————
   3. straw   ———————
   4. puddle   ———————
   5. tap   ———————
   6. gown   ———————
   7. roar   ———————
   8. eyelash   ———————
   9. Mars   ———————
  10. juggler   ———————
  11. scorch   ———————

[Observer says each word and asks the child what it means. This gives a quick clue to his verbal intelligence—his ability to decide what a word means. For example, can he say that "scorch" has something to do with fire or burning?]

Typical of a detailed conference form or "report card" for kindergartners is this:

Kindergarten Developmental Progress Record
19_____ - 19_____
Name:_____ Teacher:_____

   G=Good   I=Improving   N=Needs Improvement

Social Development	Fall/Spring
1. Respects the rights, property, and ideas of others .	———
2. Is friendly with other children	———
3. Expresses ideas and feelings within a group	———
4. Has a positive involvement in group activities	———
5. Is able to take turns	———
6. Adjusts well to new situations	———
7. Is responsible with materials and equipment	———
8. Shows self-control	———
9. Accepts responsibility	———

Visual Perception
1. Recognizes colors   _____
2. Recognizes geometric shapes   _____
3. Recognizes sizes (big, little, tall, short)   _____
4. Uses picture clues in stories   _____
5. Observes likenesses and differences in words   _____
6. Observes likenesses and differences in letters   _____
7. Left to right eye movements   _____

Auditory Perception
1. Can reproduce two- and three-syllable words   _____
2. Can count the number of sounds in spoken words   _____
3. Is able to distinguish between a long word and a short word   _____
4. Is able to recognize a sound at the beginning of a word   _____
5. Is able to recognize a sound at the end of a word   _____
6. Hears and can distinguish rhyming words   _____
7. Can recall verses and songs from memory   _____
8. Can repeat a rhythmic pattern   _____

Fine Motor Control
1. Handles scissors successfully   _____
2. Handles crayons successfully   _____
3. Handles a pencil successfully   _____
4. Able to copy geometric shapes   _____
5. Able to print first name   _____
6. Able to print last name   _____
7. Able to draw a recognizable person   _____
8. Able to write numbers and letters   _____
9. Can zip, button, and tie clothing   _____

Gross Motor Skills
1. Can hop   _____
2. Can throw a ball   _____
3. Can catch a ball   _____
4. Can bounce a ball   _____
5. Can gallop   _____
6. Can skip   _____
7. Can walk forward, backward, and sideways on a walking board   _____
8. Has awareness of direction (up, down)   _____
9. Has good balance   _____

Language
1. Expresses self spontaneously
2. Able to recall a five-word sentence
3. Able to make up simple endings for stories
4. Speaks clearly and smoothly
5. Speaks in complete sentences
6. Able to express thoughts easily
7. Can recall stories in sequence
8. Can tell a story from pictures

Arithmetic Skills
1. Can count by rote from 1-50
2. Can write numerals from 1-20
3. Knows basic shapes
4. Can use ordinals to ten
5. Recognizes numerals 0-30*
6. Can add and subtract sets through 5
7. Can order numbers 0-30
8. Has a good mathematics vocabulary (understands meaning of "equals" or "is greater than", etc.)

*child will recognize that a "2" and a "9" together are 29 before he understands the concept of 29 as a quantity of things

Reading Skills
1. Recognizes capital letters
2. Recognizes lower-case letters
3. Able to write letters of the alphabet
4. Recognizes letter sounds at the beginning of words
5. Recognizes letter sounds at the end of words
6. Attempts to sound out words
7. Recognizes own name in print
8. Recognizes classmate's names in print
9. Recognizes familiar words and signs
10. Can match capital and lower-case letters
11. Enjoys books independently
12. Likes to be read to
13. Expresses an interest in learning to read
14. Has a sight word vocabulary
15. Recognizes:
    a. Rhyming words
    b. Rhyming phrases
    c. Shapes
    d. Letters, numbers

    e. Words, phrases   _____

    f. Colors   _____

    g. Initial consonants   _____

Work Skills
1. Able to concentrate without being distracted   _____
2. Has a long attention span   _____
3. Constructively occupies time   _____
4. Is self-responsible   _____
5. Is independent and self-directed   _____
6. Follows directions   _____
7. Completes assigned tasks   _____
8. Is thoughtful and conscientious   _____
9. Accepts responsibility   _____

Communicable Childhood Diseases

In most localities, the law now requires all school children to be immunized against measles, German measles (rubella), mumps, diphtheria, and poliomyelitis. Probably your child also had an inoculation or oral vaccine against whooping cough, tetanus, and smallpox, as well as a tuberculin skin test, some time ago. Your doctor can tell you whether boosters are needed now.

Listed below are symptoms that should alert you to the possibility of communicable disease. It may be nothing more than the common cold, or it may be more serious, but if any of these symptoms appear you will be wise to keep your child at home. Although the illness may turn out to be noncommunicable, the symptoms call for medical attention. If the disease is diagnosed as communicable, you should notify the school immediately. The symptoms are:

Chills
Coughing
Diarrhea
Earache
Eyes red or running or yellowing

Jaundice (yellowing of eyes
  and/or skin)
Nausea
Runny nose
Skin eruption, sores, or rash

Fever (watch for flushed, hot face)

Glands swollen or tender, particularly about the face or neck

Headache

Sneezing

Stiff neck

Stomachache

Throat sore

Vomiting

If your doctor says the patient has any of the following diseases, keep your child home from school until he has met the conditions listed at the right:

Chicken pox	Old blisters are well crusted over, and no new ones have appeared for 72 hours. Usually 5 to 14 days.
Common cold	Cleared up at least 24 hours.
Conjunctivitis (Pinkeye)	Recovered, or doctor's certificate says noninfectious.
Diphtheria	Two negative nose and throat cultures, taken at least 24 hours apart. Usually 1 week.
German measles (rubella)	No rash or fever for 2 days. Usually about 1 week.
Hepatitis (infectious)	No fever and no jaundice. At least 1 week.
Impetigo	Free of lesions, or doctor's certificate says lesions are noninfectious. They should be covered, if possible.
Lice	Hair is free of lice and nits.
Measles	No rash or fever for 2 days. Usually 10 to 14 days.
Meningitis meningococcal	End of feverish stage or when negative cultures are obtained. Usually 14 days.
Mononucleosis (infectious)	Recovered.
Mumps	Swelling has gone. Usually 10 to 14 days.
Pediculosis	*See* Lice.
Pinkeye	*See* Conjunctivitis.
Polio	End of feverish stage. Anywhere from 14 days to 6 weeks.
Ringworm of scalp	Doctor's certificate says free of disease.

Ringworm of skin	Free of lesions or when doctor's certificate says lesions are noninfectious.
Scabies	Free of lesions or when doctor's certificate says lesions are noninfectious.
Streptococcal respiratory infections: Scarlet fever, Scarlatina, Strep throat	Recovered. Usually at least 7 days with antibiotic treatment. (Most schools insist on certificate from doctor or health department.)
Trench mouth	Recovered, with negative results from smear test.
Vincent's angina	*See* Trench mouth.
Whooping cough	No fever and no cough. At least 3 weeks.

When your child returns to school, he will be required to bring a note from you giving the reason for his absence. The school nurse may give him a brief checkup before he resumes his classroom activities.

Appendix C

Some Books Your Child Should Not Miss

The following list is by no means exhaustive, but it includes many books which, it is generally agreed among kindergarten teachers and principals, your child should not miss. You should be able to find most of them in your public library. Read them to your child, and let him "read" them to himself. Note that more than one *Mother Goose* or ABC book is included because of the great variety of illustration and treatment available. You can encourage your child's critical evaluation and judgment by helping him to notice how different artists and editors have handled the same subject.

Some of these books, such as *Mother Goose,* go far back in time. *Peter Rabbit* is now in his seventies. A. A. Milne and Wanda Gag first wrote for children in the 1920's. The thirties produced Marjorie Flack and Françoise and *The Little Engine that Could,* and Robert McCloskey appeared in the 1940's. Then there is the phenomenal Dr. Seuss, who published *And to Think That I Saw It on Mulberry Street* in 1937 and hasn't yet stopped writing and illustrating books that are matchless in their fascination for prereaders, beginning readers, and recipients of the Ph.D.

AIKEN, CONRAD. *Cats and Bats and Things with Wings.*
ALDIS, DOROTHY. *Everything and Anything.*

ANDERSON, ANN. *Old Mother Goose*.
ANGLUND, JOAN. *A Friend is Someone Who Likes You*.
ANNO, MITSUMASA. *Anno's Alphabet*.
ARBUTHNOT, MAY HILL. *Time for Poetry*.
ARDIZZONE, EDWARD. *Little Tim and the Brave Sea Captain*.
ARMOUR, RICHARD. *Adventures of Egbert the Easter Egg*.
AUSTIN, MARGOT. *Brave John Henry*.

BAILEY, CAROLYN. *The Little Rabbit Who Wanted Red Wings*.
BALION, LORNA. *Bah! Humbug?*
_____. *The Sweet Touch*.
BANNON, LAURA. *Red Mittens*.
BARTLETT, ROBERT M. *Thanksgiving Day*.
BATE, NORMAN. *Who Built the Bridge?*
BEMELMANS, LUDWIG. *Madeline*.
BERENSTAIN, STAN and JAN. *The Bears' Nature Guide*.
BERTAIL, INEZ. *Complete Nursery Song Books*.
BESKOW, ELSA. *Pelle's New Suit*.
BIRNBAUM, ABE. *Green Eyes*.
BLOOME, ENID. *Dogs Don't Belong on Beds*.
BRADBURY, RAY. *Switch on the Night*.
BRAGG, MABEL. *The Little Engine that Could*.
BRENNER, BARBARA. *Mr. Tall and Mr. Small*.
BRIDGES, WILLIAM. *Golden Book of Zoo Animals*.
BRIDWELL, NORMAN. *Clifford's Good Deeds*.
_____. *Georgie's Christmas Carol*.
BRIGGS, RAYMOND. *Mother Goose Treasury*.
BRIGHT, ROBERT. *Georgie and the Magician*.
BROOKE, L. LESLIE. *The Golden Goose Book*.
_____. *Johnny Crow's Garden*.
_____. *Ring o' Roses*.
BROWN, MARCIA. *The Little Carousel*.
_____. *Once a Mouse*.
_____. *Three Billy Goats Gruff*.
BROWN, MARGARET WISE. *A Child's Good Night Book*.
_____. *The Country Noisy Book*.
_____. *The Golden Egg Book*.
_____. *Home for a Bunny*.
_____. *The Runaway Bunny*.
BUCKLEY, HELEN. *Grandfather and I*.
BURTON, VIRGINIA. *Katy and the Big Snow*.
_____. *The Little House*.
_____. *Mike Mulligan and His Steam Shovel*.

CARLE, ERIC. *The Very Hungry Caterpillar*.
CARLSON, BERNICE WELLS. *Listen! and Help Tell the Story*.

CARRICK, CAROL. *The Old Barn.*
CHORAO, KAY. *Molly's Moe.*
CIARDI, JOHN. *I Met a Man.*
COLMONT, MARIE. *Christmas Bear.*
CONKLIN, GLADYS. *We Like Bugs.*
COONEY, BARBARA. *Cock Robin.*
CRAWFORD, MEL. *The Turtle Book.*

DAUER, ROSAMOND. *My Friend Jasper Jones.*
D'AULAIRE, INGRI and EDGAR P. *Animals Everywhere.*
DAVIS, ALICE. *Timothy Turtle.*
DE ANGELI, MARGUERITE. *Book of Nursery and Mother Goose Rhymes.*
DELAFIELD, CELIA. *Mrs. Mallard's Ducklings.*
DENNIS, WESLEY. *Flip.*
DE REGNIERS, BEATRICE. *Circus.*
———. *May I Bring a Friend.*
DUVOISIN, ROGER. *Petunia, I Love You.*

EICHENBERG, FRITZ. *Ape in a Cape.*
———. *Dancing in the Moon.*
ETS, MARIE. *Play with Me.*

FATIO, LOUISE. *Happy Lion.*
FEELINGS, MURIEL. *Jambo Means Hello* (Swahili Alphabet Book).
FISH, HELEN D. *Four and Twenty Blackbirds.*
FISHER, AILEEN. *Cricket in a Thicket.*
FITZHUGH, LOUISE. *I Am Five.*
FLACK, MARJORIE. *Angus and the Cat.*
———. *Angus and the Ducks.*
———. *Ask Mr. Bear.*
———. *The Restless Robin.*
———. *The Story about Ping.*
———. *Tim Tadpole and the Great Bullfrog.*
———. *Wait for William.*
FLANDERS, MICHAEL. *Creatures Great and Small.*
FRANÇOISE. *Gay Mother Goose.*
———. *Jeanne-Marie Counts Her Sheep.*
———. *Noël for Jeanne-Marie.*
FREEMAN, DON. *Fly High, Fly Low.*
———. *Rainbow of My Own.*
FRIEDRICH, PRISCILLA. *The Easter Bunny that Overslept.*
FRISKEY, MARGARET. *Seven Diving Ducks.*
FYLEMAN, ROSE. *Fairies and Chimneys.*

GACKENBACH, DICK. *Harry and the Terrible Whatzit.*
GAG, WANDA. *ABC Bunny.*
———. *Millions of Cats.*

GARTEN, JAN, and BATHERMAN, MURIEL. *Alphabet Tales*.
GEISMER, BARBARA PECK. *Very Young Verse*.
GOODMAN, WILLIAM. *Noah's Ark ABC*.
GOUDEY, ALICE E. *The Day We Saw the Sun Come Up*.
GRAHAM, AL. *Timothy Turtle*.
GRAMATKY, HARDIE. *Little Toot*.
GRIFALCONI, ANN. *City Rhythms*.

HADER, BERTA and ELMER. *The Big Snow*.
HAWKINSON, LUCY. *Days I Like*.
HAYWOOD, CAROLYN. *A Christmas Fantasy*.
HESS, LILO. *Rabbits in the Meadow*.
HEYWARD, DuBOSE, and FLACK, MARJORIE. *Country Bunny and the Little Gold Shoes*.
HILL, DONNA. *Ms. Glee Was Waiting*.
HOBAN, LILLIAN. *Arthur's Christmas Cookies*.
_____. *Arthur's Pen Pal*.
HOBAN, RUSSELL. *Bedtime for Frances*.
_____. *The Little Brute Family*.
HOLL, ADELAIDE, and DUVOISIN, ROGER. *Rain Puddle*.

ILSLEY, VELMA. *M Is For Moving*.

JOHNSTON, TONY. *Mole and Troll Trim the Tree*.

KEATS, EZRA JACK. *Whistle for Willie*.
KELLOGG, STEVEN. *The Mystery of the Missing Red Mitten*.
KESSLER, ETHEL. *Are You Square?*
KLEIN, HOWARD. *My Best Friends Are Dinosaurs*.
KNIGHT, HILARY. *Where's Wallace?*
KONKLE, JANET. *Schoolroom Bunny*.
KRAUS, ROBERT. *Leo the Late Bloomer*.
_____. *Milton the Early Riser*.
_____. *Owliver*.
KRAUSS, RUTH. *A Hole Is to Dig*.
_____. *The Growing Story*.
_____. *A Very Special House*.

LANGSTAFF, JOHN. *Over in the Meadow*.
LENSKI, LOIS. *The Little Train*.
_____. *Papa Small*.
LEVY, ELIZABETH. *Nice Little Girls*.
LEWIS, RICHARD. *In a Spring Garden*.
LEXAU, JOAN. *Emily and the Klunky Baby and the Next-Door Dog*.
LINDMAN, MAJ. *Snipp, Snapp, Snurr and the Red Shoes*.
LIONNI, LEO. *Inch by Inch*.
LIVINGSTON, MYRA COHN. *Moon and a Star and Other Poems*.

LONGMAN, HAROLD S. *The Kitchen-Window Squirrel.*
————. *Watch Out!*
————. *Castle of a Thousand Cats.*

MAESTRO, BETSY and GIULIO. *A Wise Monkey Tale.*
MARGOLIS, RICHARD J. *Big Bear to the Rescue.*
MATTHIESEN, THOMAS. *ABC Alphabet Book.*
McCLOSKEY, ROBERT. *Blueberries for Sal.*
————. *Make Way for Ducklings.*
————. *One Morning in Maine.*
McGINLEY, PHYLLIS. *All Around the Town.*
MEEKS, ESTHER K. *Something New at the Zoo.*
MILNE, A. A. *When We Were Very Young.*
————. *Now We Are Six.*
————. *Winnie the Pooh.*
————. *The House at Pooh Corner.*
MOORE, CLEMENT. *'Twas the Night Before Christmas.*
MORRISON, BILL. *Squeeze A Sneeze.*
MUNARI, BRUNO. *Bruno Munari's ABC.*
————. *Zoo.*

NEWBERRY, CLAIRE. *April's Kitten.*
————. *Mittens.*
————. *T-Bone and the Baby Sitter.*
NEWBERRY, PERCY. *Polly and Pete.*

O'NEILL, MARY. *Hailstones and Halibut Bones.*

PAYNE, EMMY. *Katy-No-Pocket.*
PETERSHAM, MAUD and MISKA. *Box with Red Wheels.*
PIATTI, CELESTINO. *Celestino Piatti's Animal ABC.*
POLITI, LEO. *Lito and the Clown.*
POPE, BILLY N. *Your World: Let's Go to the Zoo.*
POTTER, BEATRIX. *The Tale of Peter Rabbit.*

RAND, ANN. *I Know a Lot of Things.*
RAYNER, MARY. *Mr. and Mrs. Pig's Evening Out.*
REY, H. A. *Curious George.*
————. *Curious George Gets a Medal.*
————. *Curious George Learns the Alphabet.*
————. *Curious George Rides A Bike.*
————. *Curious George Takes A Job.*

SCHEER, JULIAN. *Rain Makes Applesauce.*
SCHNEIDER, HERMAN and NINA. *Follow the Sunset.*
SENDAK, MAURICE. *Where the Wild Things Are.*
SESYLE, JOSLYN. *What Do You Say, Dear?*

SEWELL, HELEN. *Blue Barns.*
SHARP, MARGERY. *Lost at the Fair.*
STEWART, ELIZABETH LAING. *Lion Twins.*
STOBBS, WILLIAM. *The Story of the Three Bears.*
SEUSS, DR. *And to Think That I Saw It on Mulberry Street.*
_____. *The Cat in the Hat.*
_____. *The Cat in the Hat Comes Back.*
_____. *Did I Ever Tell You How Lucky You Are?*
_____. *The 500 Hats of Bartholomew Cubbins.*
_____. *Horton Hatches the Egg.*
_____. *Horton Hears A Who.*
_____. *How the Grinch Stole Christmas.*
_____. *The King's Stilts.*
SPIER, PETER. *Fast Slow, High-Low.*
_____. *Gobble Growl Grunt.*
STEVENSON, JAMES. *Could Be Worse.*

TALLON, ROBERT. *Zoophabets.*
TENGGREN, GUSTAF. *Tenggren Mother Goose Book.*
TITUS, EVE. *Anatole.*
_____. *Anatole and the Poodle.*
TRESSELT, ALVIN. *Hi! Mr. Robin.*
_____. *Rain Drop Splash.*
_____. *White Snow, Bright Snow.*
TUDOR, TASHA. *1 Is One.*

UDRY, JANICE M. *A Tree Is Nice.*

VIORST, JUDITH. *Alexander and the Terrible, Horrible, No Good, Very Bad Day.*
_____. *My Mama Says. . .*

WABER, BERNARD. *But Names Will Never Hurt Me.*
_____. *Ira Sleeps Over.*
WEISGARD, LEONARD. *Whose Little Bird Am I?*
WILDSMITH, BRIAN. *Brian Wildsmith's ABC.*
WISEMAN, BERNARD. *Morris and Boris.*

YASHIMA, TARO. *Umbrella.*

ZACKS, IRENE. *Space Alphabet.*
ZEMACH, HARVE. *Mama, Buy Me a China Doll.*
_____. *Speckled Hen.*
ZION, GENE. *All Falling Down.*
ZOLOTOW, CHARLOTTE. *If It Weren't for You.*
_____. *Mr. Rabbit and the Lovely Present.*
_____. *William's Doll.*

Bibliography

Books: If you would like to read in greater detail about child development or about teaching principles and methods, some of the books listed here will be especially helpful. They are marked with an asterisk (*) and a brief note on the content of each.

*AMES, LOUISE BATES. *Is Your Child in the Wrong Grade?* Lumberville, Pa.: Modern Learning Press, 1978. One of the founders of the Gesell Institute of Child Development concludes that placement in a grade beyond the child's ability is one of the greatest causes of school problems.

BERSON, MINNIE PERRIN. *Kindergarten: Your Child's Big Step.* New York: E.P. Dutton & Co., Inc. 1959.

* BETTELHEIM, BRUNO. *The Uses of Enchantment.* New York: Alfred A. Knopf, 1976. A noted child psychologist hopes that "a proper understanding of the unique merits of fairy tales will induce parents and teachers to assign them once again to that central role in the life of the child they held for centuries."

* CHESS, STELLS, M.D., with WHITBREAD, JANE. *How to Help Your Child Get the Most Out of School.* Garden City, New York: Doubleday & Company, Inc., 1974. A professor of pediatric psychiatry and a

journalist who reports on child development and schools discuss how children learn, identify common problems of the early years, and offer clear and simple advice to parents.

DOMAN, GLENN. *How to Teach Your Baby to Read: The Gentle Revolution*. New York: Random House, 1964.

FRAIBERG, SELMA H. *The Magic Years*. New York: Charles Scribner's Sons, 1959.

* GARDNER, D. BRUCE. *Development in Early Childhood—The Pre-School Years*. New York: Harper & Row, Inc., 1964. Factual background on growth and change toward selfhood in the first six years.

GESELL, ARNOLD, *et al. The First Five Years of Life: A Guide to the Study of the Pre-School Child*. New York: Harper & Row, 1940.

_____, and ILG, FRANCES L., *et al. Child Development*. New York: Harper & Row, 1949.

* GINOTT, HAIM G. *Teacher and Child*. New York: The Macmillan Co., 1972. Using his familiar style of simple examples and anecdotes, Dr. Ginott demonstrates how psychology can provide effective tools and skills for teachers and how therapeutic concepts can be translated into educational practices.

HANSEN, CARL F. *The Amidon Elementary School: A Successful Demonstration in Basic Education*. Englewood Cliffs, N.J.: Prentice-Hall, Inc., 1962.

* HARTLEY, RUTH E., and GOLDENSON, ROBERT M. *The Complete Book of Children's Play*. New York: Thomas Y. Crowell Co., 1963. Guides you through your child's world of play.

HECHINGER, FRED M. (ed.). *Pre-School Education Today*. Garden City, N.Y.: Doubleday & Co., Inc., 1966.

HEFFERNAN, HELEN, *et al. Teachers' Guide to Education in Early Childhood*. Sacramento, Cal.: California State Department of Education, 1956.

* _____, and TODD, VIVIAN E. *The Kindergarten Teacher*. Boston: D. C. Heath & Co., 1960. Comprehensive coverage of the philosophy and methods of the kindergarten.

* HOLT, JOHN. *How Children Learn*. New York: Pitman Publishing Corp., 1967. Illustrates how children learn spontaneously before they become victims of the system of testing, drilling, and grading.

* _____. *What Do I Do Monday?* Greenville, Miss.: Delta, 1970. Written for teachers, excellent for parents on constructive activities and why they should be done.

* HYMES, JAMES L., JR. *The Child Under Six*. Englewood Cliffs, N.J.: Prentice-Hall, 1963. Development from birth to six, with discussion of such subjects as discipline, tantrums, and values.

LAMBERT, HAZEL M. *Teaching the Kindergarten Child*. New York: Harcourt, Brace and Co., 1958.

* LANE, HOWARD, and BEAUCHAMP, MARY. *Understanding Human Development*. Englewood Cliffs, N.J.: Prentice-Hall, 1959. Application of knowledge of human development to classroom practice.

* LEONARD, GEORGE B. *Education and Ecstasy*. New York: Delacorte Press, 1968. Eloquent plea for recognizing lifelong education as the main purpose of life and for taking advantage of the infinite creative capacity of the human brain.

MOORE, OMAR KHAYYAM. "Autotelic Responsive Environments and Exceptional Children." In *Experience, Structure, and Adaptability*, edited by O.J. HARVEY. New York: Springer Publishing Company, 1966.

———, and ANDERSON, ALAN R. "The Responsive Environments Project." In *The Challenge of Early Education*, edited by R. HESS and R.M. BEAR. Chicago: Aldine Publishing Co., 1968.

* MOORE, RAYMOND S., and MOORE, DOROTHY N. *Better Late Than Early*. New York: Reader's Digest Press, 1975. Provides considerable evidence that the child is better off at home than in school until he reaches "integrated maturity" of vision, hearing, speech,

* PINES, MAYA. *Revolution in Learning: The Years from Birth to Six*. New York: Harper & Row, Inc., 1967. From observations of Head Starters and others, some startling conclusions on pre-school learning.

PITCHER, EVELYN GOODENOUGH, and AMES, LOUISE BATES. *The Guidance Nursery School* (A Gesell Institute Book for Teachers and Parents). New York: Harper & Row, 1964.

* POSTMAN, NEIL, and WEINGARTNER, CHARLES. *The School Book*. New York: Delacorte Press, 1973. Subtitled, "For people who want to know what all the hollering is about"; directed to parents by educator-authors, who, in lively and sparkling text, pinpoint what school means and where it's headed. You'll find yourself reading this one aloud to all within earshot.

RADLER, D.H., and KEPHART, N.C. *Success through Play*. New York: Harper & Bros., 1960.

ROBISON, HELEN F., and SPODEK, BERNARD. *New Directions in the Kindergarten*. New York: Teachers College Press, Columbia University, 1967.

SMITH, MORTIMER. *A Citizen's Manual for Public Schools*. Boston: Atlantic-Little Brown and Co., 1965.

STANDING, E. MORTIMER. *The Montessori Method: A Revolution in Education*. Fresno, Cal.: The Academy Library Guild, 1962.

STONE, DENA. *Children and Their Teachers*. New York: Twayne Publishers, 1957.

* TODD, VIVIAN E., and HEFFERNAN, HELEN. *The Years before School: Guiding Pre-School Children.* New York: The Macmillan Co., 1964. How parents and teachers can organize and operate child care centers, parent co-operatives, and nursery schools.

* WANN, KENNETH D., DORN, M.S. and LIDDLE, ELIZABETH ANN. *Fostering Intellectual Development in Young Children.* New York: Teachers College Press, Columbia University, 1962. Helping children age three to six through programs built around key concepts that interest them.

* WEES, W.R. *Nobody Can Teach Anyone Anything.* Garden City, New York: Doubleday & Company, Inc., 1971. Why and how parents and teachers must change. Subtitled, "What our schools are doing *to* our children, not *for* them."

WINN, MARIE, and PORCHER, MARY ANN. *The Playgroup Book.* New York: The Macmillan Co., 1967.

Curriculum guides, from public school systems in the communities listed:

Baltimore, Maryland: *Guidelines: Early School Admissions Programs; Living and Learning in the Kindergarten*

Boston, Massachusetts: *Kindergarten Education* (general); *Mathematics; Language Arts*

Chicago, Illinois: *Guidelines for the Primary Program of Continuous Development*

Detroit, Michigan: *Developmental Activities for School Beginners in the Primary Unit; Kindergarten Is Readiness; Readiness Is Action*

Fort Lauderdale, Florida: *Kindergarten Curriculum*

Grosse Pointe, Michigan: *The Kindergarten Book; The Monteith Primary Plan*

Houston, Texas: *Guide for Teaching in the Kindergarten and Junior Primary*

Minneapolis, Minnesota: *The Early Elementary School: A Handbook to Guide Teachers*

Norwalk, Connecticut: *Pre-Reading Program,* Language Arts Department

Petaluma, California: *Kindergarten Guide*

San Francisco, California: *The Kindergarten Program; Extended Skills in the Language Arts—Primary Grades*

Seattle, Washington: *Classroom Management Suggestions; The Kindergarten Work Period; Language Arts: Kindergarten; Language Arts: Grade One; Reading Readiness Check List; Thoughtful Observances of Special Days and Weeks in the Kindergarten*

Washington, D.C.: *A Handbook of Information for Teachers in the Elementary Schools*

Wilton, Connecticut: *Language Arts Program, K-3*
Illinois Department of Education: *English Language Communication, Grades K-6*
Minnesota Department of Education: *A Guide for Teaching in the Kindergarten*

Pamphlets for parents of kindergartners, from public school systems in the communities listed:

Baltimore, Maryland
Boston, Massachusetts
Bridgeport, Connecticut
Buffalo, New York
Chicago, Illinois
Detroit, Michigan
Ferndale, Michigan
Garden City, New York
Great Neck, New York
Houston, Texas
Los Angeles, California
Madison, Wisconsin

Milton, Massachusetts
Milwaukee, Wisconsin
New Orleans, Louisiana
Niagara Falls, New York
Norwood, Ohio
St. Louis, Missouri
Seattle, Washington
Simsbury, Connecticut
Stamford, Connecticut
Washington, D.C.
Wilton, Connecticut

Other booklets:

ENZMANN, ARTHUR M. *Position Paper on Detroit's Primary Unit.* Detroit Public Schools Department of Early Childhood Education.
FULLER, ELIZABETH MECHEM. *Values in Early Childhood Education.* National Education Association, 1201 Sixteenth Street, N.W., Washington, D.C. 20036.
GABBARD, HAZEL F. *Preparing Your Child for School.* Washington: Office of Education, U.S. Department of Health, Education and Welfare.
GORE, LILLIAN, and KOURY, ROSE. *Educating Children in Nursery Schools and Kindergartens.* Washington: Office of Education, U.S. Department of Health, Education and Welfare.
GUDRIDGE, BEATRICE M. *Happy Journey.* Washington: National Education Association.
HAMLIN, ELIZABETH. *Let's Look at Kindergartens.* Washington: National Education Association.
HARRIS, DALE B. *Let's Take a Look at Responsibility.* Washington: National Education Association.
HEADLEY, NEITH. *Foundation Learnings in Kindergarten.* Washington: National Education Association.

JENKINS, GLADYS GARDNER. *The Teacher of Reading and the Primary Child*. Glenview, Illinois: Scott, Foresman and Co.

LESSER, ARTHUR. *Health of Children of School Age*. Washington: Children's Bureau, Welfare Administration, U.S. Department of Health, Education and Welfare.

MEAD, MARGARET. *A Creative Life for Your Children*. Washington: Children's Bureau, Welfare Administration, U.S. Department of Health, Education and Welfare.

MINDESS, MARY and KELIHER, ALICE V. *Advantages of Kindergarten*. Washington: Association for Childhood Education International.

NULTON, LUCY, *et al*, eds. *Children and Today's World*. Washington: Association for Childhood Education International.

RASMUSSON, MARGARET, ed. *Reading in the Kindergarten?* Washington: Association for Childhood Education International.

VERHEY, N. *Reading Suggestions and Helps*. Peterborough, N.H., Public Schools.

The First Big Step. National School Public Relations Association.

Good Morning, Teacher. Chicago Public Schools.

How Seattle Public Schools Teach Reading. Board of School Directors, Seattle, Washington.

"If Your Child . . ." District of Columbia Department of Public Health.

A Kindergarten Guide. Kindergarten Association of Connecticut.

Kindergarten Today. National Education Association.

Know Your Schools. Chappaqua, N.Y., Public Schools.

The Pre-School Curriculum of the Chicago Public Schools. Chicago Public Schools.

The Primary School. Milwaukee Public Schools.

See How They Grow. Reprint from *These Are Your Children,* a child-development text by Gladys Gardner Jenkins, Helen S. Schacter, and William W. Bauer. Glenview, Illinois: Scott, Foresman and Company, 1966.

Some Guiding Principles for the Chicago Public Schools. Chicago Public Schools.

Standards of Teaching and Learning. Seattle Public Schools.

Stevie's Kindergarten Day. National Kindergarten Association.

The Years from Four through Eleven. The Little Red School House, 196 Bleecker Street, New York, N.Y. 10012.

Your Child and Reading. National Education Association.

Your Child from 1 to 6. Washington: Children's Bureau, Welfare Administration, U.S. Department of Health, Education and Welfare.

We Are Only Five Once. National Kindergarten Association.

What Happens in Kindergarten? California Association for Childhood Education.

What Is a Good Play School? The Play Schools Association.

What! Science in the Kindergarten? National Kindergarten Association.

Periodicals:

BEEBE, M.K. "Teachers and Parents Together in an Innovative Early Education Program," *Today's Education,* September 1976.

BIXBY, A.A. "Do Teachers Make a Difference? Views of Former Kindergarten Students," *Education Digest,* September 1978.

BONE, J. "Peotone Fights School Failure; Special Classes for Kindergartners with Learning Disabilities," *American Education,* January 1977.

BOTTEL, H. "Nurtury: Male-run Nursery School," *Good Housekeeping,* July 1978.

BRANDT, RICHARD M. "Ready or Not?" *Childhood Education,* April 1967.

BRENNER, ANTON. "Re-examining Readiness," *Childhood Education,* April 1967.

CARPENTER, ETHELOUISE. "Readiness Is Being," *Childhood Education,* November, 1961.

CRAWFORD, P. "Wonderful World of the Two-Year-Old; Program at St. Andrew's Nursery School, Cherry Hill, New Jersey," *Parents Magazine,* February 1977.

CULKIN, JOHN M., S.J. "A Schoolman's Guide to Marshall McLuhan," *Saturday Review,* 18 March 1967.

DE LEON, S. "Verdict on Nursery Schools: Big on Promises, Short on Delivery," *Parents Magazine,* May 1975.

FOERSTER, L.M., "For Innovation, Kindergarten Teachers Are Where It's At," *Education Digest,* December 1974.

HAMALAINEN, ARTHUR E. "How A Child Grows," *Childhood Education,* February 1967.

HOCK, R. "Dangers of Early Emphasis on Reading," *Intellect,* March 1978.

JACKSON, S.A. "Should You Teach Your Child to Read? Preparing the Preschooler," *American Education,* October 1977.

KOVALCIK, A.L. "Another Look at Reading Readiness," *Education Digest,* September 1977.

KUETTNER, AL. "Eric Hoffer: Uncommon Ideas from an Uncommon Man," *Pace,* December 1967.

MACGINITIE, W.H. "When Should We Begin to Teach Reading?" *Education Digest,* February 1977.

MAYER, MARTIN. "What's Wrong with Our Big-City Schools?" *Saturday Evening Post,* 9 September 1967.

MOORE, OMAR KHAYYAM. "The Responsive Environments Project and the Deaf," *American Annals of the Deaf,* Vol. 110, No. 5, 1965.

O'LEARY, K.D. "How Nursery Schools Teach Girls To Shut Up," *Psychology Today,* December 1975.

PINES, MAYA. "A Pressure Cooker for Four-year-old Minds," *Harper's,* January 1967.

SCHRAG, PETER. "Kids, Computers, and Corporations," *Saturday Review*, 20 May 1967.

WRIGHT, K.A. "Do-It-Yourself Nursery School," *Redbook*, July 1977.

"7 Ways to Ready Your Child for School," *Better Homes & Gardens*, August 1978.

"If Your Child Is Starting School This Month," *Changing TImes*, September 1978.

"Which Nursery School for Your Child?" *Changing Times*, May 1976.

"The Young Child: Today's Pawn?" *Educational Leadership*, November 1965.

"Focus on Reading," *Elementary English*, March 1964.

"New Hands in Finger Paint; Hiring Men Staffers at The Nurtury, Sherman Oaks, California," *Newsweek*, 9 February 1976.

"Research," *The Reading Teacher*, January 1964. Articles on reading before Grade One.

"Pre-School and Beginning Reading," *The Reading Teacher*, October 1964.

The Christian Science Monitor. Various articles on elementary education.

Fairpress, Norwalk, Connecticut. Various articles on education.

Time Magazine. Miscellaneous articles, mostly in "Education" and "Books" departments.

The New York Times and *The New York Times Magazine*. Numerous news reports and feature stories in the field of early childhood education.

The Wall Street Journal. Various articles on education.

The Wilton Bulletin, Wilton, Connecticut. Various articles on education.

GLOSSARY

Some terms you will want to recognize as you read this book:

Cognitive behavior the faculty of knowing any item or body of information or any system or concept; the process by which knowledge is acquired.

Directionality combines with laterality to produce coordination.

Language arts reading, writing, speaking and listening.

Large muscles the arms, legs, torso.

Laterality the sense with which the mind distinguishes between the two sides of the body (left and right).

Mainstreaming including handicapped children in regular daily classrooms rather than in special class situations of their own.

Motor behavior the physical actions of the body: arms, legs, eyes, hands, fingers, feet, head movement.

Motor-sensory skills cutting and pasting etc., combined with counting or with identifying letters and words.

Motor skills the ability to control motor behavior.

Patterning, or pattern of behavior any movement which has a definite form that is repeated when a given action is repeated (e.g., hand-writing, skipping rope, throwing a ball).

Perceptual skills   the ability to perceive forms through the senses.

Readiness   that stage in a child's physical, mental, emotional, social and empirical development when he or she is able to undertake a given learning experience with ease, understanding and interest.

Science   a mode of inquiry, not a body of knowledge.

Self-concept   knowledge of one's self as an individual who is separate and distinct from the objective world.

Small muscles   fingers, toes.

Spatial discrimination   the ability to interpret the perception of forms in the conceptual relationship of space.

Index

G22141

$9.95

Ryan, Bernard, 1923-
How to help your child start school.